COUNCIL
OF EUROPE

CONSEIL
DE L'EUROPE

Project No. 12:
"Learning and teaching modern languages for communication"

Evaluation and testing
in the learning and teaching
of languages for communication

Contributions by

V. Kohonen, J. van Weeren, M. Schratz, M. Oskarsson,
M. Buckby, J. Samuel, R. Schärer, P. Mairesse

Introduction by J. Trim

D1377889

Council for Cultural Co-operation

Strasbourg 1988

Strasbourg, Council of Europe, Publications and Documents Division
ISBN 92-871-1548-6

CONTENTS

	Page
Introduction, by John L M TRIM	4

CHAPTER I   FUNDAMENTAL PRINCIPLES — 9

I.1   Evaluation in relation to communicative language teaching, by Viljo KOHONEN — 11

I.2   "On determining the function and quality of language tests", by Jan van WEEREN — 27

I.3   "On the trail of everyday experience ... The individual learner's personality as an influential factor for the development of learner-centred tests", by Michael SCHRATZ — 34

I.4   "Self-assessment of communicative proficiency", by Mats OSKARSSON. — 46

CHAPTER II   SOME NATIONAL DEVELOPMENTS — 59

II.1   "Graded objectives in relation to communicative testing and national examinations", by Michael BUCKBY — 61

II.2   "Evaluation in the educational context", by Jane SAMUEL — 77

CHAPTER III   A PROPOSAL FOR LANGUAGE EXCHANGE — 89

III.1   "A strategy for the collection, storage and exchange of assessment, evaluation and exam approaches and instruments", by Rolf SCHÄRER — 91

III.2   "Automatic data processing: an example of a system using a data base", by Paul MAIRESSE — 95

APPENDIX I

Conclusions and recommendations of the meeting of experts on testing, assessment and evaluation (Strasbourg, 26-27 June 1986) — 108

APPENDIX II

Index of contributors to the report. — 110

Introduction

In 1982 the Committee of Ministers adopted Recommendation R (82) 18 concerning the teaching of modern languages in the member states of the Council of Europe. Among the measures to be implemented, member states were urged in paragraph 2:

"to promote, encourage and support the efforts of teachers and learners at all levels to apply in their own situation the principles of the construction of language-learning systems (as these are progressively developed within the Council of Europe modern languages programme):

-   by basing language teaching and learning on the needs, motivations characteristics and resources of learners;

-   by defining worthwhile and realistic objectives as explicitly as possible

-   by developing appropriate methods and materials

-   by developing suitable forms and instruments for the evaluation of learning programmes".

In paragraph 14, member states were recommended:

"to promote the national and international collaboration of governmental and non-governmental institutions engaged in the development of methods of teaching and evaluation in the field of modern language learning".

Project 12, "Learning and teaching languages for communication", was established by the Council for Cultural Co-operation (CDCC) in 1982 and continued until 1987, its primary task being to promote the implementation of the recommendation of the Committee of Ministers. Much of the project has been devoted to the organisation, in association with sponsoring authorities in most member states, of a series of workshops for teacher trainers covering many aspects of communicative language teaching. Evaluation and assessment have figured in a number of these workshops, eg:

(84) 7 (b)   "The task-based assessment of communicative language competence"

(85) 2   "Communicative language teaching and assessment: preparing teacher-trainers to implement a new national system for secondary school pupils to age 16"

(85) 3   "Teaching of foreign languages for communicative purposes at school level (age 10-14): classroom strategies and evaluation"

(85) 4   "The assessment and testing of communicative performance in foreign languages in secondary schools (with special emphasis on in-service training)"

(85) 12   "Kits for successful communicative language learning and teaching - approaches to fluency, accuracy and assessment"

(86) 7   "Communication at work"

(86) 10   "Development of autonomy of pupils learning German (age 11-18)".

Reports on these workshops are being issued by the Council of Europe. In particular, Peter Green, Director of Studies of Workshop (85) 4, held in the University of York, has edited and developed the presentations and working papers of that workshop to produce "Communicative Language Testing: a resource handbook for teacher trainers". The handbook, containing contributions by J L M TRim, W T Littlewood, M Buckby, J Hellekant, J L Clark, E MacAogain and K W Hecht, is published by the Council of Europe.

In addition two meetings on problems of evaluation, assessment and testing in relation to the learning and teaching of languages for communication were held in Strasbourg in the framework of Project 12. At the first, the issues and problems were discussed and a number of papers commissioned. At the second, held on 26-27 June 1986, the papers were received and discussed. A number of conclusions and recommendations for future action by competent authorities were adopted. They are reproduced in this publication together with the commissioned papers.

It is no accident that evaluation, assessment and testing are regarded as an essential component of language learning/teaching systems development, but are placed in fourth position. A careful identification of the developing needs of learners is regarded as fundamental to all planning, if a language learning programme is to be worthwhile. The learners' motivations and relevant characteristics must be taken fully into account if the programme is to be appropriate. The resources which are available, human as well as material, must also be assessed if programmes are to avoid utopianism and be practicable in the actual conditions of learning and teaching. The analysis of the learning/ teaching situation in this way allows realistic objectives for a programme to be determined in the necessary detail and to be useful, appropriate and feasible. A similar realism governs the selection, or development, of methods and materials which will enable a given learner, or group of learners, to reach the agreed objectives.

If it is only at this point that the need for evaluation, testing and assessment is introduced, that is because of a fear of the "tail wagging the dog". Testing and assessment are necessary to provide the many interested parties with the information they need to take decisions in the light of their various responsibilities. Learners and employers need to know whether the learner's communicative proficiency is adequate to his or her communicative needs or demands. Learners and teachers need to know what to build on when a course begins. During a course they require to monitor progress towards the agreed objectives. Teachers and educational authorities need to know whether courses are successful in reaching their objectives, or whether weaknesses are revealed that need to be corrected. Without feedback, no process can be effectively controlled.

However, established tests and examinations may begin to lead an independent existence and to dominate the learning/teaching process. Learner needs and objectives both become "to pass the examination and gain a qualification" and teachers come to see their responsibility in the same way. Materials and methods are then judged according to their effectiveness in preparing candidates for examinations. The tests are then evaluated according to psychometric, logistic and financial criteria. If the contribution of one participant to the quality of communication cannot be realiably assessed (and who can tell which hand is responsible for the success or failure of clapping?) so much the worse for communication as an objective! Again, the received criterion of discrimination demands the widest possible spread of candidates. If all do well, the test "fails" to discriminate and should be rejected. Accordingly, tests will tend to address areas of marginal proficiency and emphasise the differences between candidates. If norm-referencing is employed with tests with high discrimination, a set proportion of candidates will appear to have done very badly, even though their achievement may in fact be considerable. The achievement common to all candida es is taken, as it were, for granted and brushed aside as undeserving of credit. Undue importance is attached to formal correctness, which gives an illusion of objectivity, although analyses of conversation show that spontaneous interaction through speech is often fragmentary, marked by false starts and changes of direction and construction in mid-sentence leading to errors in agreement, word order, etc. Indeed, experienced users of a language are accustomed to exploit their knowledge of its properties to penetrate through to the communicative intention of the speaker and to react appropriately to that intention. They disregard, and are often unaware of, the minor ways in which the speaker's utterance diverges from the well-formed sentence they reconstruct. A simple test will demonstrate the principle. Once you are well-launched into a conversation, ask your partner to repeat what he has just said, or what you have just said. The reaction is likely to be one of surprise and perhaps irritation, followed by reflection and then, in most cases, a rephrasing which preserves the meaning, but not the form, of what was originally uttered. Any hesitations, stammering, repetitions and minor errors will be edited out, as they generally are when people commit their thoughts to writing. Most people will be considerably taken aback when confronted with an accurate transcription in writing of what they have said, not only in conversation but in, say a lecture delivered without notes. Speech which comes across as fluent and well-structured to the ear appears disjointed, repetitious and ill-formed to the eye. Non-native speech which is accepted by listeners as of near-native quality seems full of infelicities, even errors, when written down. Under examination conditions, this may mean that the same level of performance is likely to be evaluated highly in an impressionistic oral examination, but severely penalised as a written production.

The consequence of these differences between spoken and written language present those responsible for evaluation, assessment and testing with difficult dilemmas. Justice demands objectivity. How can something so fugitive, transitory yet complex as spontaneous conversation be objectively assessed? Especially by an examiner who is expected to be a participant as well as an observer and judge? How can success or failure in communication be ascribed to one or another party? What confidence can one have that in a brief encounter, probably

with a stranger, performance is determined by the essentials of proficiency
rather than by the accidentals of the unique here-and-now, the relation
established in a potentially high-stress situation? While these question
marks remain, then when serious matters are at stake - employability, entry to
professions or to higher education - it is not surprising that authorities
feel more comfortable in their accountability when able to present evidence for
their judgement in marked written texts, assessed according to an exactly
quantifiable scheme. How much safer, more reliable, the computerised marking
of multiple-choice items appears to be, or the meticulously graded penalisation
of errors in a carefully constructed passage for dictation or translation!
The apparent combination of quantifiability and intellectual rigour is almost
irresistible. To advocate the replacement of such well-tried procedures by
impressionistic assessments of a contribution to communicative interaction in
a competition where everybody gets a prize can easily appear to be a "trahison
des clercs", an abandonment of standards and flabby liberalism. Yet, as we
know, the ability to perform intellectual exercises to order is no measure of
ability and willingness to engage in the unpredictable, risky business of the
meeting of minds. Classroom practice which is dominated by such exercises
alienates a high proportion of learners and actively inhibits the development
of communicative skills.

These tensions are felt most keenly in systems which are driven by public
examinations. It is no coincidence that the issue of public examinations and
testing has played a much larger role in the workshops organised in the United
Kingdom than elsewhere. The paper by M Buckby in this collection gives a clear
account of the attempts now being made in England and Wales to resolve the
issue along lines very similar to those being followed in the separate Scottish
system (cf Workshop (85) 2), but different in many ways from those reported for
France by J Samuel. The basic principles of the communicative approach appear
now to be widely accepted among all the interests involved in language teaching
- inspectors, publishers, examiners, teacher trainers as well as classroom
teachers themselves. The replies to questionnaires sent to participants in the
37 workshops show near unanimity in this respect. From what has been said
above, the reader may well - and rightly - conclude that in applying the
principles to language teaching on a national scale, problems of assessment
and evaluation may be of crucial importance.

In papers presented here, J van Weeren concentrates attention on the
function of testing as "the process of delineating, obtaining and providing
useful information for judging decision alternatives" and develops quality
criteria for the evaluation of tests in relation to their function. This
perspective is important, since it enables us to tackle such questions as: for
what purposes is self-evaluation appropriate? How may learners be sorted into
effective working groups? What different roles have teachers to play in testing
for different purposes?

V Kohonen takes a more general look at the relations between teaching and
evaluation in a communicative approach, emphasising the positive role of
evaluation in providing the learner with "feedback about the development in his
skills, rather than pinpointing minor errors in his performance", looking to
tests to encourage communicatively oriented classroom work.

M Schratz, concerned as to how testing can be reconciled with the principle of learner-centredness, which is basic to the Council of Europe's approach to language teaching, pleads for an "integral" testing procedure, which will avoid creating an artificial division between the test situation and the preceding tuition and take proper account of the "communicative attitude" of the learner, closely related to his individual personality and feeling of identity. He sees self-assessment as the ultimate objective, a theme explored in greater depth by M Oskarsson, whose previous work on the subject for the Council of Europe is well-known and influential.

In a final section R Schärer and P Mairesse propose a strategy for international co-operation in the collection, storage and exchange of information regarding approaches and instruments used in testing, assessment, evaluation and examinations, showing how a database, such as that currently being developed by the Eurocentres organisation, could be used for this purpose.

At their meeting on 26-27 June 1986, having received and discussed the paper presented here, the group of experts made a series of suggestions addressed to authorities responsible for examinations and tests in member states and to the Council for Cultural Co-operation. It is hoped that these recommendations, reproduced here in an Appendix, together with other Council of Europe documentation in this area and the papers collected here, will be of assistance to the language teaching profession in understanding and tackling the problems of evaluation, as an integral part of the learning and teaching of languages for communication.

J L M Trim
Project Advisor

CHAPTER I: FUNDAMENTAL PRINCIPLES

I.1 EVALUATION IN RELATION TO COMMUNICATIVE LANGUAGE TEACHING

by Viljo KOHONEN
University of Tampere, Finland

This paper will first discuss aspects of education, evaluation and communication. Communicative competence is seen as a multi-faceted phenomenon consisting of two types of knowledge, declarative and procedural knowledge, and of four sub-competences: grammatical, pragmatic, functional and socio-linguistic competence. It is suggested that communication is a "graded" property that is possible at various levels of accuracy. If the development of communicative skills is seen as a continuum ranging from zero communication to virtually bilingual competence, learners can be encouraged to work towards the quality of skills that is within their reach. More attention should be paid to internal evaluation aimed at improving the learning process. The development of self-directed, autonomous learning is seen as a challenge in language education.

1. Views of education, communication and evaluation

1.1 Evaluation to improve learning

A thought-provoking distinction has been made by Bloom (1981) between two major functions of education: that of selection, and that of developing learner talent. Bloom points out that education has traditionally had a selective function, whereby the basic task of education has been to identify those who can be permitted to enter secondary and thereby higher education. In this view, a central task of education is to classify learners into various "streams", under the assumption that they are different and the school must select those who are capable of academic education.

The selective function is, of course, still one task of school. But Bloom argues that it has become less important in developed societies in which a major proportion of the age group completes secondary education and there is an increasing demand for education for all citizens in a complex society. In this situation, education has as its primary function the development of the individual. A central task of education is to develop those characteristics in all students which will enable them to live effectively in a changing society. Thus the school should devote major resources to increasing the effectiveness of individuals rather than to predicting and selecting talent:

Education must be increasingly concerned about the fullest development of all children and youth, and it will be responsibility of the schools to seek learning conditions which will enable each individual to reach the highest level of learning possible for him or her (p. 3).

Bloom further points out that the rapid change in modern society requires education to continue throughout life. In a similar way, Wragg (1984) notes that education is, in fact, based on a vision of the future for which learners are prepared. To serve such needs, he suggests a multi-dimensional view of the curriculum which will foster the following kinds of learner properties:

- creativity: capacity for imaginative and inventive thinking

- social and inter-personal skills: ability for co-operative work

- study skills: capacity for autonomous learning, involving the learner's responsibility for his own learning and the idea of life-long education.

Hemming (1984) suggests the notion of a "confidence-building curriculum", which involves the following elements of successful education: promoting the learner's curiosity for learning, encouraging him to face challenging experiences, and building up his confidence to take risks. If the learner withdraws from formative interactions and learning opportunities he cannot utilise his potential fully. Education should involve the whole child, his feelings, intellect, interests and purposes and provide experiences of success "in proportion to effort". Active, learner-involving participation yields valuable and lasting learning experiences by tapping the learner's whole person. Contributing effectively to the process will increase his self-esteem and develop his confidence The teacher has a significant role in acting as a stimulator, facilitator and guide in the process.

On the basis of the role of evaluation in the total curriculum, it is possible to distinguish between three philosophies of evaluation: the selective, criterion-referenced and what could be called "learner-supportive" evaluation (cf Warries 1982). The central question is what the learner's performance is compared to: whether that of his peers, a pre-defined mastery level, or his previous level of learning.

The selective philosophy is, of course, well-known to all teachers and is based on differential psychology and the statistical trend for the "normal" distribution of human abilities in large groups. It is connected with the selective function of the school. What is considered an excellent, moderate or poor performance is to some extent at least determined by the empirical distribution of the scores. By definition, an "excellent" performance by some learners implies less excellent performance by some others. One can ask what are the affective consequences of such comparisons for the less able learners (cf Bloom 1971a), and how necessary the comparisons really are in school. While information about the rank order is necessary for various placement, selection and streaming purposes, it is not needed at the classroom level.

In the criterion-referenced philosophy, the learner's performance is compared with a required level of mastery, based on the objectives of instruction. Instead of competing with his peers, the learner competes with the teaching

objectives (cf Takala 1985, Carroll 1971, Bloom 1971b, van der Linden 1982).
This philosophy represents a significant improvement in educational thinking.
Learning is seen as an individual effort of the learner towards the objectives.
There are, however, some shortcomings: the definition of the behavioural domain
is problematic, as is the definition of the required level of mastery (cf Carver
1974, Cziko 1981, Takala 1985). Further, in school conditions with fixed
numbers of teaching periods available, it seems unavoidable that a number of
learners will not reach the mastery level, while others will (or at least should)
go beyond the common objectives.

This is where the third, learner-supportive philosophy of evaluation would
seem to offer some promising possibilities. In this approach, the learner
"competes" with himself, to reach his personal objectives and augment his
learning in comparison with his previous level of learning. This is essentially
what Blook seems to suggest in his second view of education: enabling each
individual to reach the highest level of learning possible for him. This
thinking leads to autonomous learning whereby learners take on "learning
contracts" that are reasonable within their total learning situations. In a
sense, any learner who has efficiently utilised his potential is a "good" learner.
This suggests bigger contracts for fast learners and smaller ones for slow
learners. Such contracts are based on their responsibility for their own
learning and thus gradually lead to an attitudinal growth towards their being
autonomous learners.

It is perhaps impossible, and even undesirable, to define exactly what
"efficient" use of the potential means. It can be seen as an unfolding potential
which depends on genetic and environmental factors. It refers to the learner's
total learning situation and includes ability factors, learning opportunity,
home and school support, and the individual's needs and motivation (cf Strevens
1980). We should beware of labelling our learners, as teacher expectations may
involve well-known "self-fulfilling prophesies" (cf Rosenthal and Jacobson 1968,
Elashof and Snow 1971, Rosenthal and Rubin 1978, Babad et al. 1982). We could
rather aim towards an open-ended, basically supportive view of our learners and
encourage them to go as far as they wish and are able to go in their learning,
within the possibilities allowed by their total learning situations. What is
important is the teacher's trust in the learner, and an unconditional acceptance
of him as a person regardless of his performance level in school.

1.2 Communication as a "graded" property

The skills involved in communication can be examined in the light of a
model of communicative competence. The model adopted is multi-faceted, involving
two types of knowledge: a "declarative" knowledge of the rules of the language,
and their "procedural" use in actual communication. The distinction and the
various sub-competences can be illustrated by the following figure (cf Canale
and Swain 1980, Canale 1983, Faerch et al 1984, Faerch 1986):

COMMUNICATIVE COMPETENCE

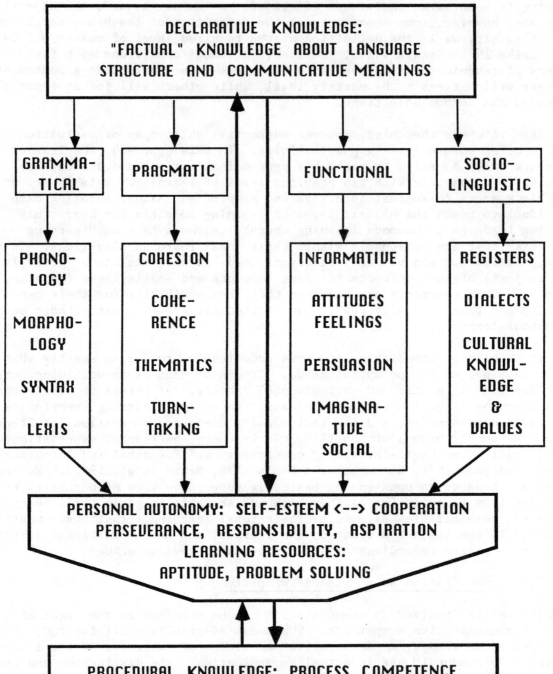

Declarative knowledge is factual knowledge about the systematic structure of language and includes a knowledge of communicative functions and socio-linguistic aspects of language use. Grammatical competence refers to **accuracy** at the various levels of linguistic description. At the discourse level, pragmatic competence is concerned with the **well-formedness** of utterances and texts with respect to cohesion, coherence and thematic structure, as well as turn-taking in conversation. The keyword in the description of functional competence is **purposefulness** of communication in terms of different communicative functions, while socio-linguistic competence refers to **acceptability** in communicative situations, depending on who talks to whom, about what and in what situation. These components are intertwined in actual communication, but their analysis as separate sub-competences helps one to realise that communicative competence involves much more than mere grammatical accuracy.

Procedural knowledge, by contrast, is language performance in various contexts of actual language use. It can also be described as implicit, internal-ised and contextualised knowledge. It may not be readily available for conscious reflection of rules and thus need not be consciously monitored. We can also talk about skill learning, which proceeds from the explicit, cognitive stage to an autonomous stage, where access to the knowledge is rapid and automatised. Automatisation is significant from the processing point of view, as it relieves short-term memory capacity for the processing of the message contents (cf Anderson 1985).

An interesting and controversial question is how procedural knowledge develops and what kinds of memory representations the learner has at different stages of learning. Krashen (1982, 10-11) makes the well-known distinction between acquired and learned knowledge. For him, "acquisition" is unconscious and leads to implicit knowledge, while "learning" is conscious and yields explicit knowledge. Such a distinction is, however, artificial, and Krashen pushes it so far as to claim that learned knowledge will not become acquired, but is available to the learner only through conscious monitoring. Therefore he rejects traditional rule-dominated language teaching and emphasises the importance of communicatively meaningful language use: "language teaching should focus on encouraging acquisition, and providing input that stimulates the subconscious language acquisition potential all normal human beings have (1982, 83).

It makes perhaps more sense to assume that declarative and procedural knowledge constitute a continuum, where rules may have conscious memory representations in varying degrees, being partly explicit, partly implicit. Faerch (1986, 126) suggests the following stages on such a continuum from implicit to explicit rules: (1) the learner uses the rule but does not reflect on it -> (2) he can decide that speech is/is not in accordance with the rule -> (3) he can describe the rule in his own words -> (4) he can describe the rule in metalinguistic terms. A communicative use of language results in implicit knowledge, while presentation of rules yields explicit knowledge. But the latter type of knowledge can become implicit through automatisation, just as implicit knowledge can become explicit through consciousness-raising. This two-way process can be illustrated by the following figure (Faerch 1986, 127):

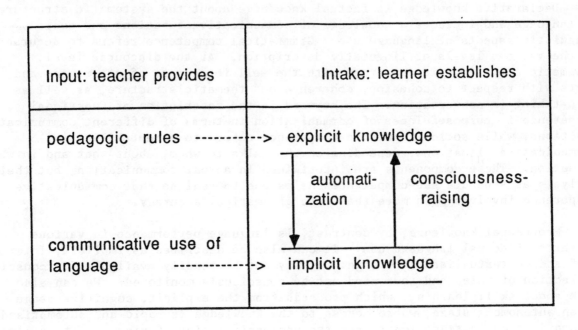

Input: teacher provides	Intake: learner establishes
pedagogic rules ---------->	explicit knowledge
communicative use of language ------------>	implicit knowledge

Teaching can variously emphasise different skills and explicit or implicit knowledge, depending on the objectives and the communicative needs of learners. Traditionally, emphasis has been on explicit knowledge and written language, resulting in less fluent language use. A prerequisite for fluency is implicit knowledge. Its development requires communicative language use. Learners need to be provided with rich experiences in personally meaningful and relevant uses of language, producing messages of their own.

The growth of process competence is connected with the development of declarative knowledge: increasing structural and lexical knowledge will enable the learner to express more complicated ideas as well. This yields an increase in the learner's communicative resources. Obviously, modest needs can be satisfied to some extent with very limited skills. In tourism contexts, for example, mere non-verbal communication and limited vocabulary and ready-made phrases are already helpful. However, communicative teaching objectives must go beyond a mere "phrase-book" stage of communication. Thus every learner does need some grammatical knowledge, whether explicit or implicit. Grammar can be regarded as a "map" of the language, helping the user to get a grasp of the systematic linguistic structure and thereby utilise the inherent redundancy. Redundancy utilisation, ie the ability to anticipate structures and meanings in discourse, is an important component in fluency. It is also necessary to have some knowledge of culturally acceptable behaviour in the target country, ie what is appropriate language use in different contexts. Language use is not just a matter of knowing words and forming proper sentences; it is also a tool of international sharing and understanding.

Language errors hamper communication and may cause it to break down in more serious cases. Such «breakdowns» are not, however, fatal in spoken contexts, as the interlocutors usually have a possibility to ask for clarification - just as we do in mother-tongue communication as well. It seems to be deficient lexis and basic syntax that hamper comprehension more than inaccuracies in pronunciation or morphological forms (cf Littlewood 1984; Dulay et al 1982). Accuracy is obviously the goal to work towards, but it is not an end in itself. Equally important is that learners have something to say and the courage to use the language, even at the risk of making mistakes.

In an important sense, communication is also a matter of taking risks and learning to cope with unpredictability. Communicative competence includes an element of communicative self-confidence. This point is also made by Dulay et al, who point out that «All things being equal, the self-confident, secure person is a more successful language learner» (1982:75). Our teaching should therefore allow room for the development of communicative risk-taking attitudes and strategies as well. Relatively modest language skills are already useful if the learner has the courage to use them. But learners also need to be given demanding tasks that challenge them to work at the frontiers of their current skills, being «pushed», as it were, to extend and stretch their communicative repertoire, in terms of both receptive and productive skills. We should create «communicative pressures» in the classroom, providing learners with opportunities for risk-taking in a safe environment - as the saying goes, «nothing ventured, nothing gained»! Coping successfully with problems will enhance the learner's self-esteem and his communicative confidence and thereby foster his growth towards autonomy in language use. As teachers we need to invest professional thinking in the quality of the learning tasks, examining critically what kinds of skills and attitudes they develop in the learners.

Communication can thus be seen as a «graded» property that is possible at various levels of accuracy. While all learners need some amount of grammar and vocabulary, not all learners need to achieve a perfectly accurate command of the foreign language. Accuracy and the internalisation of the systematic structure of the target language are a direction to work towards. For some learners accuracy is a feasible and important goal, while some others might realistically set their accuracy objectives at more modest levels or even aim at quite specific objectives.

Learner communication is also a «graded» property. Even though learners work on the same objectives in classroom contexts, it is obvious that not all of them will reach the same level of communicative skills within the same amount of instructional time - there will always be learners for whom languages are easy and those for whom they are difficult. Thus they will end up with various levels of proficiency at the end of school. It is particularly the abstract rule system that poses difficulties for slow learners, while fast learners are still able to acquire both accurate and fluent language skills. Now, communicative thinking would seem to offer a possibility for reconciling instructional objectives and variation in learner ability. If accuracy may not be reached by all learners, everybody should be able to communicate **something** in the foreign language nonetheless. Some acceptable level of communication should be within everybody's reach. Thus slow learners can - and should - be given credit for comprehensible and acceptable language. But by the same token fast learners should be required to attain high standards of accuracy, and they can be encouraged to work to this end. This means, then, accepting different outcomes for different learners, depending on their ability (and motivation) to learn languages. In any case, we should aim at developing effective communicators who have the courage to enter interaction and use language at whatever level of accuracy and comprehensibility.

2. Evaluation in communicative language teaching

2.1 Learning, teaching and evaluation

In a broad sense, evaluation can be understood as a continuum ranging from informal classroom observation to formally administered, standardised tests. Its purpose is to produce samples of learner language, yielding empirical data for making various inferences and instructional and educational decisions. The choice of formality levels, types of tests and item contents depends on the objectives of testing, ie, what kind of information is desired from the learners for a given purpose. The model of communicative competence discussed above suggests a close connection between language learning, teaching and evaluation. Teaching can be seen as a process whereby opportunities are created for learning, and evaluation provides information for instructional and educational decisions. Teaching can facilitate student learning by providing relevant input, encouragement and feedback. But the teacher's input has to become the learner's intake, and this process takes place in the learner's cognitive structures. It requires an active participation by the learner in the learning process. Nobody can learn anything for anybody else.

The model of communicative competence suggests a multi-faceted view of evaluation. The data of learner language can be «hard», ie, carefully designed and administered tests of various language skills, and «soft», ie, data collected using techniques such as introspection, observation, field notes, interviews, diaries, questionnaires, and audio and video recordings. Data can be collected to make inferences about various aspects of the learner's declarative knowledge of the target language: what kinds of «rules» the learner has, and how these are modified in the course of his learning. An intriguing question is the development of procedural knowledge and the role of automaticity in the process. This is a research-oriented view of language learning and evaluation, but the research work need (and, indeed, should) not be left to researchers alone: every teacher can also be a researcher of his own work, posing questions and making observations and notes about classroom events and thereby deepening his professional understanding of the processes. There can be an integral relationship between teaching and evaluation, whereby evaluation can provide information for instructional decisions.

A distinction can be made between internal and external evaluation (cf Murphy 1985, Potts 1985, Lewkowicz & Moon 1985). Internal evaluation is process-oriented and provides information for monitoring the ongoing learning process. This information gives feedback to the teacher about the progress of learning in the class and thereby helps him to plan his instructional procedures. For the learner, internal evaluation gives information about how he is progressing. External evaluation, by contrast, is product-oriented performance testing, aimed at gauging the learner's skills in tasks which

represent those for which he is preparing (cf Hauptman et al, eds. 1985).
Such tests may be administered by the teacher as summative tests, or by
educational authorities for purposes of getting feedback of the curriculum,
or for placement or selection purposes. From the learning point of view,
it seems that more professional thinking needs to be devoted to the
development of internal evaluation, as this can have a powerful effect on
shaping the ongoing learning process.

2.2 On internal evaluation by the learner

The central question in internal evaluation is how to monitor the
learning process and thereby improve the quality of learning. For the
learner, such information provides guidance as to where he stands in his
learning task: what he can already do with this language communicatively,
what rules he masters, what are his strong points and weaknesses, and how
he has progressed in comparison with his previous stages of learning. Such
information will increase the learner's awareness of his own learning.
Internal evaluation can have a significant role in the internalisation of
the criteria of language use and correctness.

Helping the learner to manage his own learning is largely a question
of increasing his awareness through training. Feedback mechanisms can be
built in the learning process to provide learners with information about
how they are proceeding in their learning tasks. Such mechanisms include a
wide range of possibilities: introspection, self-assessment,
questionnaires and check-lists, learner diaries, peer assessment, various
recordings, and formative tests designed specifically to yield information
about the progress of learning. The aim is to help learners to become more
successful language learners by learning to monitor their own processes
and developing repair strategies to compensate for weaknesses in their
communicative skills. Learners can be trained to observe and monitor their
own learning, thereby becoming, as it were, «researchers» of their own
learning. As learning proceeds the teacher's role becomes less prominent,
with more responsibility being shifted to the learner for his own progress.
Learning how to learn is an important educational aim in a changing society.

2.3 On external evaluation

External evaluation is concerned with predictive validity: how
successfully the examinee will be able to communicate in certain target
situations. This is the product-oriented view of learning. As the main
interest is placed on performance, the diagnostic value of external tests is
usually smaller. When designing external communicative tests aimed at giving
marks in school reports, the following questions can serve as a useful
checklist:

i.   What to measure? The central question is, what we mean by «knowing a
     language» and how we operationalise our views in concrete tests,
     in other words what is the test's view of language. Summative tests
     will inevitably indicate what we regard in our syllabuses as «worth
     learning». In communicative thinking this must be essentially the
     ability and willingness to put into communicatively meaningful use
     whatever amount of language the learner has acquired. Tests must
     therefore be designed so that they give the learner opportunities
     to show what he can do with his language. This brings in the

requirement of authenticity or, in any case, an attempt to
simulate real-life tasks of language use. Information must be
provided about the audience, setting and purpose of the test
tasks, and the scoring criteria. While testing is always
artificial to some extent, we can attempt to reduce artificiality
as far as possible.

ii. What kinds of tests to use? Communicative skills can be measured
by various kinds of tests, calling into play different aspects
of communicative abilities. Various types of tests are necessary
in order to gain a many-sided coverage of the skills involved.
Any single test type (or a limited number of types) will inevitably
give a narrow measure of the skills. We should not lose sight of
the communicative relevance of the tests. This is also important
because of the well-known backwash effect of tests on teaching:
our testing procedures should encourage communicatively oriented
classroom work.

In terms of the distinction between discrete-point (analytic) and
integrative (global) tests, analytic tests could be used as formative
tests of the learners' knowledge of the discrete points of grammatical
structures. Integrative tests, on the other hand, would be better
suited as summative tests, enabling learners to show what they can do
with their language skills. Communicative thinking thus suggests the
use of integrative tests as a measure of communicative abilities. This
would provide a communicatively balanced basis for giving marks in the
school reports.

iii. At what level of mastery? Following the familiar Bloomian
taxonomy (cf also Takala 1985), language processing can be thought
of in terms of three levels:

- recognition of language items, understanding of meanings
- mechanical skills, limited recall, guided production
- creative, autonomous use of language in communication

Recognition of discrete structural forms and meanings by answering
multiple-choice items is, of course, a relevant part of language competence,
but this is rather a limited view of the variety of the language skills
needed in real-life contexts. Such contexts will typically require
open-ended, personal interpretations of meanings. Besides, if we think of
language processing as a creative reconstruction of meanings, we have to
provide open items to measure such skills. Perhaps comprehension can be
measured more directly by open tasks, since a learner who is able to answer
open questions will usually pass multiple-choice items as well, while the
converse is not necessarily true (cf Anderson 1985). In this sense open
questions are more economical, as they measure language processing at a
more demanding level.

iv. How to score learner productions? Scoring problems are bound to
arise in mixed-ability groups where learner responses will scatter
over a wide range in terms of both the quality and quantity of
language. To cope with the variation in productive tasks, some
scale is necessary; mere 0/1 will not do justice to all. Besides,
communicative thinking suggests that language use is not a simple
«wrong/right» matter; messages can usually be expressed in a
number of possible ways, and what is involved is rather a scale
of acceptability and communicative efficiency. The basic criterion
for the application of the scale must be comprehensibility:
has the learner understood the gist of the text? or would a speaker
of the target language understand the intended meaning? If the
answer is positive - despite incorrect spelling and grammatical

mistakes - the learner has managed to interpret or process the message successfully and deserves some credit for it. Obviously, a zero will be given for a blank answer as well as for an answer that is clearly not interpretable. Thus, on a scale 0 - 3, for example, 3 points will be given for a «perfect» answer, 1 point for a comprehensible attempt, and 2 points for a variety of combinations of partly incorrect language and deficient message contents.

v. How to transform the scores into marks? Communicative thinking leads to a criterion-referenced orientation, with communicative efficiency and the degree of attainment of the objectives as the criteria. The specification of the mastery level is a difficult task, and the application of the criteria to the evaluation of the learner performance is always a matter of subjective interpretation. This entails problems of reliability. It is well-known that validity and reliability are difficult to maximise in the same test. Thus, for example, while multiple-choice items eliminate problems of scorer reliability, their validity is limited as a measure of the communicative use of the foreign language. Validity must be given the first priority in communicative testing. On the other hand, any communicative test must also meet sufficient requirements of reliability in order to be a valid measure of anything.

In school contexts, evaluation usually involves a conversion of the scores into some scale of marks in the school reports. As noted above, norm-referenced evaluation is less important within the class and school - society, and higher institutions will need such information only in school-leaving reports. More important than learner comparisons is the tenet that evaluation can be geared to improving student learning.

It seems very difficult to convert the learner-supportive evaluation philosophy into any commensurable scale of numerical marks that could be applied consistently to all learners in mixed-ability groups. The philosophy suggests self-assessment by the learner himself and thereby a shift away from numerically evaluated learner performance. One possibility for converting the scores into school marks within a somewhat loose criterion-referenced orientation would be to describe the pass marks at three broad levels of performance:

1. pass level («basic» objectives)
2. functionally satisfactory level («common» objectives)
3. autonomous level («extended» objectives)

For the lowest pass marks, accuracy is less important as long as communication meets satisfactory standards in comprehensibility, acceptability and relevance, while accuracy is an increasingly important criterion for the highest marks, involving autonomous and fluent language use. Fast learners will thereby be encouraged to work both for accuracy and fluency. They can take on more demanding learning contracts by aiming towards qualitatively higher standards of language use.

3. Discussion

When a foreign language is taught to the whole of the age group, learner performance will be automatically «graded» in terms of both the quality and quantity of the language understood and produced, as it is in the mother tongue communicative skills as well. On the other hand, communication is also a «graded» property in the sense that it is possible at a variety of accuracy levels. Errors will variously hamper communication, but language is so redundant that it tolerates a fair amount of misuse before communication really breaks down. Besides, in normal interactive situations, it is usually possible for the interlocutor to check his comprehension by asking. Language use is a matter of negotiating about meanings based on shared knowledge (cf Widdowson 1979). Successful communication also requires communicative risk-taking, a courage to attempt interaction.

Perhaps it is helpful to make a distinction between language teaching and testing in the sense that while teaching should also be prescriptive, ie, giving normative rules about accurate and acceptable language use, testing could be descriptive. Teaching would thereby have accuracy as an aim, but performance testing could be more concerned with gauging what the learner can do with his language in communicative contexts. Thus accuracy is not to be seen as an end in itself, but rather as a tool for efficient communication.

These ideas about learner variation and communication could lead to an approach encouraging learner autonomy, whereby different learners take on different learning contracts in terms of both the quantity of contents and the quality of language skills aimed at. Thus fast learners should be encouraged to work for both an accurate and fluent command of the language, thereby utilising effectively their potential for learning the abstract rule system. For slow learners, on the other hand, it would seem equally advisable to attempt to put into communicative use that amount of language which is within their reach, thereby giving them positive experiences of being able to use the language in a comprehensible and meaningful way. If communication is a relative concept, everyone can be encouraged to proceed as far as possible within his total learning situation. How far such an approach can be realised in practice depends on the constraints imposed by classroom realities and teacher education. But this would seem to be a possibility that is worth exploring.

A second important point is the role of affective factors in language use. Language use also involves an element of ambiguity, tolerance and risk-taking. Comprehending unheard (and unseen) messages and producing one's own messages also requires communicative confidence, perseverance and willingness to attempt communication. If such attitudinal aspects are to be learned in school, we need to think of pedagogical ways of developing them in classroom work. A problem with testing is that attitudinal attributes do not easily lend themselves to reliable measurement; besides, setting up authentic communicative situations is laborious and thus expensive. But considerations of economy and quantifiability should not dictate our testing procedures, if we want to be serious about measuring communicative aspects of language use in realistic target contexts. Validity should be given the first priority in testing, as long as care is taken to ensure sufficient reliability at the same time. In practice we have to make compromises due to existing resources. But such compromises should be made with a professional consideration of what could be done, and how much of it can be done with available resources.

A further important point about communicative testing is that it should
not undermine the learner's self-confidence and discourage his attempts
to use the language. We can aim at giving him positive feedback about the
development of his skills, rather than pinpointing minor errors in his
performance. Concentration on errors will put into focus what the learner
does not know, thus leaving aside the important aspects of what he already
knows and how much he **can** communicate in the foreign language. Communicative
testing allows room for both «hard» and «soft» aspects of evaluation.
Summative tests will inevitably tell learners what we regard as «worth
learning», and they will exercise a powerful backwash effect on teaching.
Our tests can encourage communicatively oriented classroom work.

In mixed-ability groups, tests can be adapted for differences in
learner performance. In the present approach (cf Kohonen 1983, 1985), the
notion of «graded tests» refers to the design of the items ranging from
recognition to creative production. Emphasis is shifted into integrative
skills, thus enabling learners to show what they can do with their language.
A second important point is that learners are encouraged to proceed as far
as they can. They can attempt to solve the items as far as they wish. This
is in accordance with our conviction to avoid imposing limits on learner
performance. Grading is thus tactful, something that takes place automatically
in the learner's mind when he sees that he cannot solve the items any further.
(Cf Harding et al, 1980).

Communication is not just a matter of knowing the language system.
It is just as importantly a matter of having something to say and the courage
to attempt communication. There are numerous possible and acceptable ways
of sharing in cross-language communication. It is our task as teachers to
help our learners to find **their** ways and get positive learning experiences
from their discovery of the foreign language.

Bibliography

Alderson, C (ed), 1985. Evaluation. Lancaster practical papers in English
        language education, vol. 6, New York: Academic Press.

Altman, H & V James (eds), 1980. Foreign language teaching: meeting
                individual needs. New York: Pergamon Press.

Anderson, J R, 1985. Cognitive psychology and its implications.
        San Francisco: W H Freeman and Company.

Babad, E Y et al, 1982. «Pygmalion, Galatea and the Golem: investigations
                of biased and unbiased teachers». Journal of Educational
                Psychology 74, 459-74.

Block, J (ed), 1971. Mastery Learning. New York: Holt, Rinehart & Winston.

Bloom, B, 1971 a. «Affective consequences of school achievement». In
        Block, J (ed) 1971, 13-28.

Bloom, B, 1971b. «Mastery learning». In Block, J (ed) 1971, 47-63.

Bloom, B et al, 1981. Evaluation to improve learning. New York:
            McGraw-Hill.

Canale, Michael, 1983. «From communicative competence to communicative
            language pedagogy». In Richards, J C & R W Schmidt (eds)
            1983, 2-28.

Canale, Michael & Merrill Swain, 1980. «Theoretical bases of communicative
                        approaches to second language teaching and
                        testing». Applied Linguistics 1, 1-47.

Carroll, J B, 1971. «Problems of measurement related to the concept of
            learning for mastery». In Block, J (ed). 1971, 29-46.

Carver, R P, 1974. «Two dimensions of tests: psychometric and edumetric».
            American Psychologist 28, 512-18.

Cziko, G A, 1981. «Psychometric and edumetric approaches to language
            testing: implications and applications». Applied Linguistics 2,
            27-44.

Dulay, H et al, 1982. Language Two. New York: Oxford University Press.

Elashof, J D & R Snow, 1971. Pygmalion reconsidered. Worthington:
            C A Jones.

Faerch, Claus, 1986. «Rules of thumb and other teacher-formulated rules in
            the foreign language classroom». In Kasper, G (ed) 1986,
            125-43.

Faerch, Claus et al, 1984. Learner language and language learning.
                Copenhagen: Gyldendals Sprogbibliotek.

Harber, C et al, 1984. Alternative educational futures. New York: Holt,
            Rinehart & Winston.

Harding, A et al, 1980. Graded objectives in modern languages. London:
                Centre for information on language teaching and research.

Hauptman, P et al (eds), 1985. Second language performance testing.
                Ottawa: University of Ottawa Press.

Hemming, J, 1984. «Confidence-building curriculum». In Harber, C et al
            1984, 13-26.

Johnson, K & D Porter (eds), 1983. Perspectives in communicative language
                teaching. New York: Academic Press.

Kasper, G (ed), 1986. Learning, teaching and communication in the foreign
            language classroom. Aarhus: University Press.

Kohonen, V, 1983. «Learners, teachers and graded objectives in communicative
            language teaching». In Nyyssönen, H & A Mauranen (eds)
            1983, 37-67.

Kohonen, V 1985. «Testing communication skills in mixed-ability groups».
            In Kohonen, V & A J Pitkänen (eds), 1985, 91-108.

Kohonen, V & A J Pitkänen (eds), 1985. Language Testing in School.
                        AFinLA Yearbook 1985. AFinLA Series of
                        Publications No. 41. Tampere.

van der Linden, W J, 1982. «Criterion-referenced measurement: its main
                applications, problems, and findings». Evaluation in
                Education 5, 97-118.

Lewkowicz, J & J Moon, 1985. «Evaluation: a way of involving the learner».
                In Alderson, C (ed) 1985, 45-80.

Littlewood, W, 1984. Foreign and second language learning. Cambridge: CUP.

Murphy, D F, 1985. «Evaluation in language teaching: assessment,
            accountability and awareness». In Alderson, C (ed) 1985,
            1-17.

Nyyssönen, H & A Mauranen (eds), 1983. AFinLA Yearbook 1983.
                        AFinLA Series of Publications No. 36.
                        Oulu and Helsinki.

Porter, D, 1983. «Assessing communicative proficiency: the search for
                validity». In Johnson, K & D Porter (eds) 1983, 189-209.

Potts, P J, 1985. «The role of evaluation in communicative curriculum, and
            some consequences for materials design». In Alderson, C (ed) 1985,
            19-44.

Richards, J C & R W Schmidt (eds), 1983. Language and communication.
                        London: Longman.

Rosenthal, R and L Jacobson, 1968. Pygmalion in the classroom. New York:
                Holt, Rinehart and Winston.

Rosenthal, R & D B Rubin, 1978. «Interpersonal expectancy effects: the first 345 studies». The Behavioural and Brain Sciences 3, 377-415.

Strevens, P, 1980. «The paradox of individualised instruction: it takes better teachers to focus on the learner». In Altman, H & V James (eds) 1980, 17-29.

Takala, S, 1985. «Criterion-referenced testing in foreign-language teaching». In Kohonen, V & A J Pitkänen (eds) 1985, 9-32.

Warries, E, 1982. «Relative measurement and the selective philosophy in education». Evaluation in Education 5, 191-203.

Widdowson, H, 1979. Explorations in applied linguistics. Oxford: OUP.

Wragg, T, 1984. «Education for the twenty-first century». In Harber, C et al 1984, 1-12.

I.2 ON DETERMINING THE FUNCTION AND QUALITY
OF LANGUAGE TESTS

―――――――――

by Dr. Jan van WEEREN
National Institute for Educational Measurement
(Cito), The Netherlands

―――――――――

This paper deals in a rather informal and concise way with basic aspects of testing, such as test functions and factors that determine test quality.

An attempt is made to formulate some simple and straight-forward criteria that can be used for the evaluation of language tests in general and «communicative» language tests in particular.

1.   Test functions

Evaluation, assessment and testing are related terms in the field of education. However, «evaluation» would seem to be a much friendlier term than «testing». The word «testing» has come to have rather unfavourable connotations like «stress», «errors», «bad marks» and «failure». From a more scientific point of view, «testing» simply refers to a specific type of evaluation,whereas «assessment» only denotes a part of the evaluational process.

The nowadays already classical definition of educational evaluation goes as follows: it is **the process of delineating, obtaining and providing useful information for judging decision alternatives.** The first step of an evaluational procedure is the indentification of useful information for decision making. «Obtaining» refers to the technical aspect of gathering valid and reliable information. This information should be provided in such a way that decision making is made as easy as possible. Finally, the decision alternatives can entail all the aspects of an educational setting, eg the objectives (Should we try to include objectives a, b, c in the curriculum and/or leave d, e, f out?), the course (Should we spend more time on subject x or not? Should we favour exercises of the y-type or rather exercises of the z-type?) or the teacher (Should (s)he be more or less authoritarian with these specific groups of learners?).

Testing is conveived of as a special type of evaluation. With testing the decision making refers individuals. Decisions are made about the careers of learners.

Assessment emphasises the act of judging. It presupposes the gathering and processing of relevant data, but the term would not seem to imply decision alternatives other than alternative qualifications: good and bad marks, positive or negative judgments.

Learner-oriented decisions are essentailly instructional decisions. The decision alternatives consist of different treatments or learning processes that learners have to go through. According to Van der Linden (1983) instructional decisions can be reduced to four basic types: MASTERY, SETTING, STREAMING and SELECTION. They can be represented by different flowcharts:

Figure 1

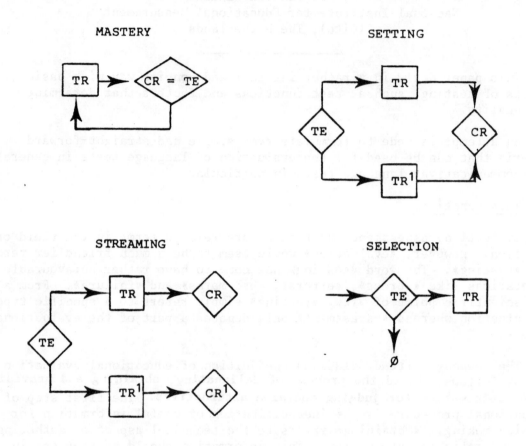

There are three basic notions in these flowcharts: the «test» TE, the «treatment» TR and the «criterion» CR. TR stands for a specific course and CR refers to its objectives.

Four kinds of test-based decisions are possible:

In the case of MASTERY it has to be decided whether a testee can proceed or has to repeat one or more parts of the course.

SETTING or placement means that a testee will be offered the most suitable treatment out of two or more alternatives. (S)he may either proceed slowly or quickly, with much teacher support or rather independently. This will depend on his or her abilities, experience or previous knowledge. The main point is that every learner will attain the same objectives in the end, that learning outcomes will be approximately the same for all.

STREAMING or classification implies that not only the treatments differ but also the criteria: different testees will get a different treatment in order to attain different objectives.

SELECTION, finally, is a very familiar decision type: will the testee be admitted to a course or institution or will (s)he be rejected?

Instructional decisions are generally based on recurrent or iterative assessment procedures. Pupils are given qualifications for their work at certain intervals; these qualifications will accumulate to a statement about their mastery of the learning content, about their attainment of the intended course objectives: is their degree of mastery sufficient or not, can they be moved up or will they stay down?

Recurrent assessment of achievement, of learning success provides the learner with regular feed-back. It is a form of stimulating learning efforts. Although instructional decision making is the original aim, the **ultima ratio** of testing as it were, testing often appears to be confined to simple assessment and people management. However, if genuine test functions are to be fully articulated and exploited, tests must have specific properties. The following function-related properties are considered important:

Mastery decisions: the test is an operationalisation of the course objectives. Therefore it is a straightforward achievement test. Normally, a substantial majority of the candidates will have attained the objectives after completing the course. The main question is: who has succeeded and who has failed? No rank ordering of candidates is required. Only one level, the level of sufficient mastery, has to be defined in operational terms.

Setting decisions: the test will have a diagnostic character. Ideally, the test output should be an analysis or profile of the learner's language proficiency as well as a description of his or her learning ability or style. Language testing and psychological testing go hand in hand.

Streaming decisions: candidates are distributed over different streams, normally on the basis of the level of command already attained (which is by no means the worst predictor of success in language study!). The candidates must be ranked with the greatest possible reliability. Cut-off scores for admittance to a certain stream will regulate the distribution of candidates: only those with a score of, let's say, at least 545 will be admitted to the higher stream. All the others can enter the lower stream, unless their score is below 515; these candidates will have to take a special course. Like selectional decisions, streaming decisions are rather arbitrary. They tend to depend on the accidental intake capacity of different streams. The mechanism of supply and demand will play an important part.

Selectional decisions: the test must rank the candidates according to their level of achievement or proficiency. Precise discrimination between the weak and average or, alternatively, between the average and good candidates is required. Discrimination between the weak and very weak or between the good and very good is of less importance. The former category will simply be rejected, the latter simply admitted. As for the average students decisions may vary. Depending on the available intake capacity of an institution or other criteria it will either reject only the weak and very weak candidates or admit only the good and very good ones.

As a rule, the function of familiar test-types can be described under the heading of one of these decision types. A university entrance examination, for example, entails selectional decisions. The well-known TOEFL-test (Test of English as a Foreign Language) is essentially an instrument for streaming decisions, more or less according to the following flowchart:

TOEFL

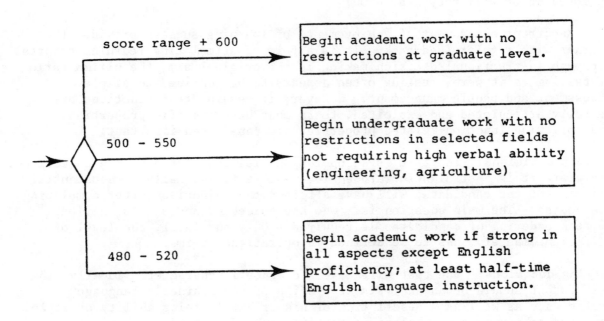

score range ± 600	Begin academic work with no restrictions at graduate level.
500 - 550	Begin undergraduate work with no restrictions in selected fields not requiring high verbal ability (engineering, agriculture)
480 - 520	Begin academic work if strong in all aspects except English proficiency; at least half-time English language instruction.

Candidates will get different treatments with different objectives depending on their TOEFL-score. Some of them will take subjects that require high verbal ability, eg English literature; others will go for more scientific subjects like physics. A sub-group first will have to take an English course with specific objectives.

Classroom tests designed with a view to improving the learning process also range among standard decision types. For example, the so-called diagnostic test provides information that enables the user to take decisions of the mastery or setting type: the learner can either proceed, or will have to repeat parts of the course, or: (s)he will have to go through a sub-class A or B of exercises (different treatments) in order to meet the criterion.

Graded tests are difficult to allocate. They seem to be of the mastery type: the information provided tells you where the learner stands, as it were, what (s)he has mastered.

However, there are no proper decision alternatives. As a rule, every learner can proceed. Only in extreme cases is it decided that a learner should repeat parts of the learning content.

2. Test quality

If a test is administered in order to determine, for example, (degrees of) mastery, it must be designed in such a way that, with every testee and objective, it can be decided in a reliable way which of them have succeeded in attaining the objectives and which have not.

Take, for instance, the following objectives:

* The candidate is able to take part in a foreign language conversation about a general topic by making several intelligible, meaningful and linguistically acceptable contributions of sustained speech.

* The candidate is able to understand a written text about a general subject, not requiring specific background knowledge, taken from a newspaper or a magazine, that would pose no problems if translated into his or her mother tongue.

The question is: how many conversations in which the candidate is involved do we have to observe in order to be able to say with any certainty whether or not the candidate has attained the level of proficiency first mentioned? Or, regarding the second objective: how many texts will the candidate have to read with understanding and how many questions about a text will (s)he have to answer correctly before (s)he will get the credit of having achieved the intended level of reading comprehension? In principle, the range of conversational situations or texts to be presented is infinite. Practicality, however, necessitates the introduction of the concept of REPRESENTATIVE SAMPLE. Only a sample of the learner's language behaviour is observed which is considered representative of the objective aimed at. The technical term for this representativity is CONTENT VALIDITY. The content validity of a sample of language behaviour can be assessed empirically by comparing the outcomes of the observations of one sample with those of another. If both samples are supposed to be representative, even if they are different, and the observational outcomes are similar, then either sample is assumed to be representative.

The expression «similar» is used instead of «the same». There will always be some fluctuations in the observational outcomes, due to the inaccuracy of the observational technique, the inevitable error of measurement.

Differences may also occur as a result of personal features of the candidates. Or, as Underhill (1983: 129) puts it: «Personalities differ to the extent to which they are able to focus their minds on a topic outside their particular interests. There is, in other words, a spectrum of individuals ranging from those who can apply their full mental and communicative energy to any task, to those who can only apply themselves when their particular interests are under discussion».

The magic words in this context are REPEATED OBSERVATION or REPEATED MEASUREMENT. If we are to accommodate different observational outcomes to a «real» value, an average must be calculated from our observations of the candidates who are successively performing different tasks. All these tasks should of course represent the objective under consideration. They may consist of different conversations in which the candidate has to play a certain part or of different texts (s)he has to read. Alternatively, they may focus on the quality of separate contributions made in a conversation or on the answers to separate reading comprehension questions about a text.

The more these separate moments of observation contribute to, or rather confirm an overall finding or impression, the more reliable the entire procedure is. CONTENT VALIDITY AND TEST CONSISTENCY ARE BOTH ESSENTIAL TO TEST RELIABILITY. Test consistency is normally expressed by statistical coefficients between 0 and 1 like Cronbach's Alpha or Kuder and Richardson's formulae 20 or 21.

There is yet another reliability factor, particularly where the assessment of language behaviour in a conversation (the first specimen objective) is concerned. Reading comprehension can be assessed by means of multiple choice questions, but the assessment of oral proficiency, of necessity, involves subjective rating. How can we guarantee that a rater really assesses the quality of the language behaviour shown? How can we be sure that this assessment is reliable? To what extent can we account for it? There is always a chance that a rater bases his assessment not only on the quality of the language behaviour but also on the material, political or ethical content of the testee's contributions in a conversation, be it deliberately or inadvertently. Secondly, one rater may consider the testee's social competence to be constitutive for the quality of his or her language behaviour - does (s)he let a partner finish? Aren't his or her statements too blunt? - whereas another rater may not do so. Furthermore, a testee of an average level will make better impression in a conversation after a candidate who performs poorly than after a very fluent fellow student. On the other hand, a rater may «adjust» his norms involuntarily to the average level of a certain group of testees.

Several measures can be taken in order to improve the quality of a rating procedure, including the following:

*   giving precise definitions of the different aspects of the
     language behaviour that should be taken into consideration;

*   supplying accurate definitions of the qualifications that can
     be given, eg of the points of a rating scale;

*   providing samples of (fragments of) language behaviour with the
     corresponding qualifications;

*   instruction, training and supervision of raters.

The positive effect of these measures can be determined in an empirical way. First, by assessing the STABILITY of the rating procedure: have a rater judge the same (recorded) performance of the same testees on different occasions after a certain interval of time. The ratings should be approximately the same. This so-called intra-rater reliability is normally expressed by a correlation coefficient. Secondly, by assessing the INTERSUBJECTIVITY of the procedure: have a group of raters judge the same testees' performance. Again, ratings should be similar. Inter-rater reliability can be determined by calculating intraclass correlations. Stability and inter-subjectivity both constitute the RATER RELIABILITY of an assessment procedure. A high rater reliability determines to a large extent the accountability of a rating procedure. We can guarantee a testee that the rating of his or her performance is, at least to a certain degree, independent of irrelevant and arbitrary characteristics of a rater.

However, subjective rating will always involve a certain amount of unreliability, due to lack of power of perception or flagging concentration among raters. Sources of rater unreliability can be reduced by adding more raters and averaging their ratings of the same testees.

3. Test evaluation

The following checklist for test quality can be set up; the first point is rather self-evident for all tests. The second is considered specific for communicative language testing; the third, fourth and fifth follow from the considerations presented above.

* Are the OBJECTIVES of the test clearly stated? Is it possible to deduce both the task and the evaluational criteria from the objectives?

* Does the format of the test elicit a form of language behaviour that makes sense outside the classroom? Can the task be considered a SIMULATION of relevant and functional language behaviour in a life-like setting?

* Is the test set up according to the principle of REPEATED OBSERVATION or repeated measurement? Does the test provide a number of mutually independent occasions that enable us to evaluate the language behaviour elicited according to the same criteria, each time starting «with a clean slate» as it were? For example: a test format that enables us to evaluate each turn of a candidate in a conversation separately, thus yielding a number of independent value judgments, is in principle superior to a procedure that is confined to a few impression marks at the end.

* Are the EVALUATIONAL CRITERIA well defined? Is the meaning of every possible global or analytic value judgment or mark sufficiently explitit? Have any examples of ratings been supplied?

* Last but not least: Has the TEST FUNCTION been specified? Is there a clear relation between the function and the properties of the test? For example: Is it a criterion referenced test with passing and failing scores for the assessment of mastery, or a norm referenced test, ranking the learners from highest to lowest for streaming decisions?

4. References

Van der Linden, W J (1983), «Decision Theory in Educational Research and Testing», in: Research Methodology. Volume of International Encyclopedia of Education: Research and Studies, Oxford.

Underhill, N (1983), «Common sense in Oral Testing»; in: E W Stevick a.o. (eds), On TESOL '82, Washington.

I.3 ON THE TRAIL OF THE EVERYDAY EXPERIENCE ...

THE INDIVIDUAL LEARNER'S PERSONALITY AS AN INFLUENTIAL FACTOR FOR THE DEVELOPMENT OF LEARNER-CENTRED TESTS

by Dr. Michael SCHRATZ
University of Innsbruck, Austria

who dedicates this paper to the memory of Professor Friedrich SATZINGER, who died on 4 August 1986, for his outstanding contribution to the promotion of modern language teaching in Austria and to the work of the Council of Europe Modern Languages Project.

Contents

1.   Preliminary thoughts

2.   The realm of personal experience, and its place in testing communicative performance

      2.1 Language competence

      2.2 Social competence

      2.3 Personal competence

3.   Towards an evaluation concept for the development of learner-centred tests

4.   From self-identification to self-assessment as the eventual objective.

References

Bibliography

1. Preliminary thoughts

Passing qualitative judgements on testing from the individual learner's point of view is always a delicate matter. In the case of foreign language testing the problems of assessment are intensified. The more communicatively oriented the testing items are «structured» the fewer - technically speaking - «instruments» are available. If innovative test designers suggest a complete openness of communication situations, this also means that the traditionally important criterion «objectivity» cannot be achieved. Therefore it is unfortunately not sufficient to develop testing items systematically and be stringent in our argumentation. The factors and variables involved are too manifold and disparate. In addition, there are the controversial positions which have been adopted on the testing of foreign language competence, and the no less contradictory evaluations of teaching tactics and organisational measures in schools (for example examination regulations and the like) and other educational institutions.

2. The realm of personal experience, and its place in testing communicative performance

If in this contribution I nevertheless intend to show that communicative testing is the better choice compared to any itemised structuring of testing batteries according to certain language problems, I wish to demonstrate, on the basis of my own investigations, new insights into the individual learner's role in a testing situation, and to sketch out possible conclusions to be drawn from the experience thus gained (1). Detailed principles of the underlying concept cannot be set out here, as we are at the moment concerned with the evaluation of foreign-language proficiency, which can be expressed in terms of the following declaration:

> «Dass i eben echt das sagen kann, was i mir denk, dass i des
> aussabring, aber net, dass i schon beim zweiten Wort schon
> überlegen muss: Was heisst das, das weiss i nimmermehr, was
> das heisst ... Das ist mein Problem, auf jeden Fall ...» (2)

These remarks, quoted here in isolation, were made by a participant in an English course for adults, and highlight one of the central problems of foreign-language testing: to be able to say, to want to say, to permit oneself to say in English whatever one would, in one's inner self, actually like to say. Prompted by such questions, the extensive investigation on which this contribution is based (cf Schratz et al 1983) concerns itself primarily with the extent to which the communicative testing of proficiency in the foreign-language programme for adults is capable of providing solutions for the fundamental problems of evaluative measures in a teaching institution.

In order to examine the individual learner's competence in successfully handling foreign language encounters, it is necessary to obtain more detailed knowledge of what makes him/her react in a certain way. Our investigations at once brought to light first indications of the necessity of giving serious consideration to the learner and his real, if often hidden, feelings, especially those involving his self-esteem. A lack of self-confidence, for example, can easily destroy the language competence built up in the course of the learning process. Therefore it is, in any event, important in structuring a testing procedure to take up the latent needs of the participants and pursue them hand in hand with those objectives more directly related to the language performance.

In order to submit the test dialogues on the subject of British and American affairs, once analysed, to an interpretation of their content which would allow conclusions to be drawn as to the efficacy of the underlying teaching strategies, we first of all investigated the (linguistic) behaviour of the learners and compared it with observations made in the classroom. As the learning and use of a language is decisively influenced not least by atmosphere, emotions and the level of mutual confidence, the subjective impressions of the learners gave further insight into the testing matter.

From the more than 2,000 quotations obtained in detailed analysis of these interviews, we were able, by means of a system of non-linear evaluation («brain-patterning») (3) to identify thematic focal points in the context of a framework of interpretation which made the problem of identity in the use of the foreign language («I speak English, do I?») the starting point for further deliberations (4). The points of emphasis revealed in the course participants' statements, and shown in the diagram below, mark out those areas

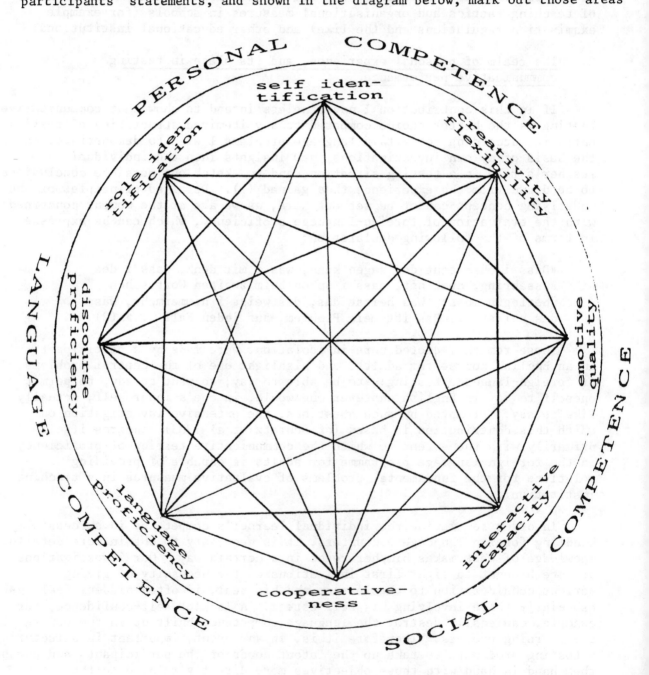

of language-teaching practice which throw particular light on the problems of orientation to the identity of the individual in foreign language testing. From all this, there emerged key words which characterise these thematic focal points. They appear in the diagram above, which also shows the manner in which they refer to the domains of competence to be achieved by the learner.

The segments of conversation connected with these key words were each subjected to a process of interpretation within the thematic complex in order to arrive, by means of the comparative analysis of individual cases, at a recognition of the general in the particular. In this way, a «learner history» was obtained from the individual interviews which, with the aid of the analysis of the central problems of foreign-language acquisition, together with the individual findings, can be reconstructed into an impressive portrayal of learner experiences characterised by practical knowledge, within the framework of a comprehensive contribution to education. Thus the interview data, taken as a whole, contribute to the construction of a social reality which is of great significance, in the first instance in the field of actual teaching in the foreign language class, but in its wider implications for the testing of a learner's overall competence gained through individual learning processes.

In order, even in a short contribution such as this, to convey some understanding of the key words and expressions contained in the diagram above, I would now like, by way of example, to summarise the main ideas behind it concerning the three domains of competence to be achieved by the learners.

2.1 Language competence

Traditional practices in the «examination» of language competence have been criticised against a backdrop of the development of the notion of capacity to act in the (foreign) language. Traditional tests cannot, according to this criticism, measure this capacity, as the influence and processes which arise in the course of a conversation cannot be reproduced within the confines of a written framework. In order to conform to the principles underlying the notion of capacity to act in the foreign language, however, an approach has to be chosen which includes a number of aspects specific to research findings in (linguistic) pragmatics (cf Edmondson/ House 1981).

As far as phases of silence are concerned, learners in communicative courses should be able to act with as few breakdowns in communication as possible. In our survey participants in communicative courses were able to act without breakdowns in ccommunication for 95% of the test period, whereas in the tests carried out in the traditional courses, the proportion of time in which an uninterrupted flow of communication was achieved amounted to only 75%. In the same way, participants in the communicative courses were able to elaborate on their speech intentions to a significantly greater degree. The average length of time spent talking about a particular topic was 1 minute and 54 seconds as compared with a corresponding figure of only 27 seconds in tests in the traditional courses.

2.2 Social competence

Whenever disruptions occur in a foreign language encounter social competence is necessary from the individual learner's point of view to restore the flow of communication again. This concerns the ability of the learner to maintain a convincing unity between individual speech intentions and co-operative arrangements in everyday situations. At the centre of the discussion is the question of whether the learner is also able to realise his ordinary self using the foreign language as his linguistic medium in contacts with others in an authentic language encounter.

Seen from the social aspect of language acquisition it is mainly a matter of interaction between the speakers involved. The multitude of chances in interacting during the learning process has a very strong formative effect on the social competence of the individual. The stricter this socialisation is marked by a linear development in the language acquisition phase the less one can speak of «social competence» in the sense we mean it.

In a test phase a competent language user may be faced with a not yet developed, or not yet fully developed ability to use the foreign language in a social context. In the learner this inner conflict is a more or less conscious process, which strongly influences the learner's language performance in foreign language testing. The respective contributions in this connection of the self and of outside influences have a more or less disruptive effect on the encounter with the foreign language. Its causes lie in a certain pressure felt by the learner to use the language in a rather limited way, since he or she does not feel at ease with the challenge of communicating in a social context.

Thus the function of the language comes, for them, to lie in their personally experiencing the communicative character of an assessment in appropriate interactive contexts, that is a process of mutual evaluation. A «socio-communicative opening-up» along these lines of the arrangements for learning a language should allow the learners scope for experiment, to feel «at home» in the foreign language and to gradually bring into play their own problems, fears and inhibitions.

2.3 Personal competence

If one proceeds from the assumption that the texts and materials contained in traditional tests do not provide a suitable basis for the independently determined expression of speech intentions in the foreign language, and that the lack of relevance of the content to the day-to-day reality of learners diminishes their motivation, then it is clear that tests of this kind create few opportunities for self-identification on the part of the individual learner. This is all the more the case as the means of expression (thus far) learned in the foreign language are not sufficient to cope (in the accustomed manner) with everyday situations. Learning experiences of this kind lead, via the phenomena of a negative self-evaluation, to self-disqualification when it comes to assessing one's personal abilities, and to the destruction of self-confidence in one's present and future capacity to use the foreign language.

In communicatively oriented tests learners should be enabled to bring
into play, at the levels of both content and interaction, their own
experiences of life and learning. By this means, they are able to evaluate
their own ability to learn, and to structure it accordingly. By way of a
series of related metaphases, and with the opportunity to bring their own
problems into play in coping with the approach to the target language,
learners are sensitised to the language acquisition process. Appropriate
content and opportunities for interaction within a test will prevent the
creation of a divide between language use on the one hand and reality and
the real substance of the practical knowledge and experiences of the learners
on the other, while at the same time increasing the latter's room for
manoeuvre. The increased account taken of factors related to the emotions
and the personality aims to bring about a discovery of identity which will
in turn enable a more creative approach to be made in language
activities.

The constructive involvement of the learner at the levels both of the
process and of the end product expands the potential of assessment in terms
of learning experiences, and this helps at the same time to promote a sense
of identity. In this way, learners in a test adopt strategies to put its
content and methods at the disposal of their own learning processes, thus
increasing their independence and sense of identity, that is to say their
ability to think, act and speak independently.

3.   Towards an evaluation concept for the development of learner-centred
      tests

The effects of the attention paid to reinforcement of the learner's sense
of identity can also be seen in the encounter with the reality of the foreign
language at home or abroad, for the participant in the course has learned
to say what he thinks and what he wants to say. It is on this level, too,
that the guidelines for future evaluation of foreign-language proficiency lie.
They must in any case have regard to the matter of coming to terms with
primary socialised learning and linguistic experiences which affect both
the individual and relations between individuals. They must, however, also
aim at the gradual development of autonomy in both the individual and the
collective learning process. This would allow realisation of the capacity to
act in the foreign language, in other words, the identification of the learner
in an assessment phase with his own learning potential as part of the process
of growth in the foreign language.

For the evaluation of communicative competence, it proves necessary
to develop a procedure capable of encompassing profound experiences in the
language-acquisition process such as may be inferred from the learner's remarks
quoted on page 2, while at the same time not neglecting phenomena in the
supra-linguistic domain. For it is only through knowledge of the ideas of
all those involved (teachers as well as learners), concerning not only those
aspects of language teaching specific to learning, but also of a wider nature
related to the life history of the individual, that it becomes possible to
link suitable forms of testing for the target group to the actual needs of
the learners and examine them as to their usefulness.

The demands made by communication in a foreign language are strongly related to overall patterns of human behaviour, so that the socio-psychological and intercultural factors to which the methods used in any test must also be geared, need to be given consideration. Moreover, within a homogeneous group of learners, differences, some of them considerable, will emerge in respect of teaching and learning behaviour. These differences are related to the life histories of the individuals concerned. This is particularly the case in connection with the previous experience of schooling and assessment respectively, which have a very definite status in the teaching and testing procedures.

In order to avoid the presentation of a diminished picture of the effects achieved by a communicatively-oriented test and the claims made for it, something which could have occurred if the investigation into this matter was reduced to concentrating on single aspects - for example by the itemisation of answers to a questionnaire - the method to be adopted is that of the qualitative research paradigm (5). Such an approach is aimed at recording the segment of reality under investigation in its entire complexity and with the greatest possible diversity. With this in mind, individual statements taken from personal experience should be drawn upon to bring out associations from the realm of daily life relevant to an interpretation of the conditions governing behaviour in the testing of a foreign language.

When in 1948 Lasswell summarised the process of communication in the question «Who says What in Which Channel to Whom With What Effect?» (Bryson 1948, 37), he offered a model which can successfully be adapted to the analysis of the specific situation of testing communication in the foreign language. Using this idea and taking into consideration the intentional educational setting one could arrive at the following:

The answer to the ten-fold question

WHO tests WHOM on WHAT by WHOM WHEN and WHERE through

WHICH media for WHICH purpose with WHICH effect?

sets the frame within which test constructors and the testers working with the tests have to legitimise their decisions.

Therefore testing is always a decision-making affair, which I want to elaborate by means of the following graphic presentation:

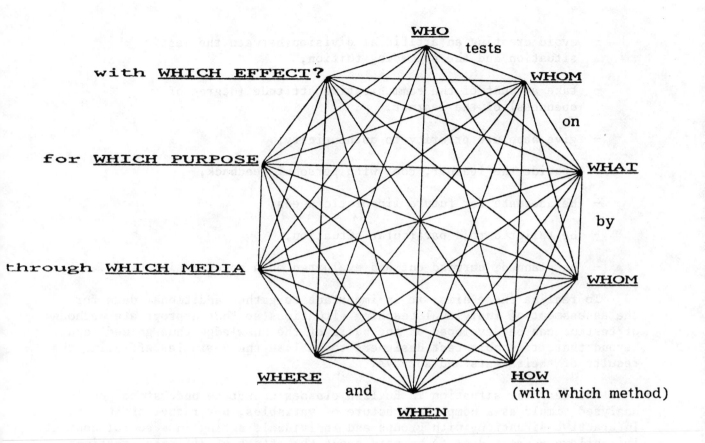

There is no doubt, of course, that these ten aspects of the question formulated into the thesis mentioned above do not refer to equivalent constituent parts of the testing procedure. In certain educational systems, for example, only the »Who tests whom?» question may be open to decision-making in planning a test. In this case one refers to an external or so-called «standardised» system whereby the concepts of validity, objectivity and reliability criteria have great weight in the rating of such tests. And yet each test or battery of testing items construct their own social reality of what is «significant» for the tester, for the institution, or society (cf Berger/Luckmann 1966). The more official value is expected from a test, the more questions in the graph have to be externally predetermined.

In other instances, usually more informal ones, it is the tester (teacher) who decides to test somebody or something (s)he has set up with a certain method at a certain time in a certain situation through the media chosen for a certain purpose. It is, last but not least, the effect on the individual testee that the tester cannot foresee in the planning. For it not only depends on the educational setting but more so on the relationship between tester and testee (usually teacher and learner) and the identity of the individuals involved.

The qualitative orientation of testing procedures should make it increasingly possible to place the emphasis in the acquisition of a foreign language on learner identity. This may be formulated in terms of the key question «I speak English, do I?» (cf 4). In order to meet the demands of dynamic research at the practical level, testing of the level of learning success has to be carried out in an **integral** procedure, designed to:

- avoid creating an artificial division between the test situation and the preceding tuition,

- take account of the communicative attitude (degree of openness) of the learner,

- give absolute priority to authenticity,

- provide the learner, too, with personal feedback,

- be adequate for future linguistic needs,

- be tailored to a particular situation,

- be planned, carried out and evaluated on a co-operative basis.

To realise these aims, it is important to gather additional data for the assessment of individual teaching situations so that appropriate methods of testing can be developed on the basis of the knowledge thus gained, and, beyond that, to enable test designers to analyse the variables affecting the results of their tests and surveys.

The learning situation in English classes cannot be understood and analysed simply as a complex structure of variables, but rather as an interactive situation, with groups and individuals acting in a social context. This allows a great deal to be said about the effect of different testing strategies on the identity of the learner, and this in turn allows comparisons to be drawn with patterns of behaviour in the learning situation. In this respect, foreign-language teaching must lead to an encounter with the unfamiliar, to a coming to terms with and explanation of it until it becomes part of oneself.

4. From self-identification to self-assessment as the eventual objective

In traditionally oriented tests, it is, without exception, attitudes to learning handed down through the ages which are revived, and this has a negative effect on primary motivation and the assessment by the individual of his own abilities. A form of testing which follows a rigid strategy, taking formally (gramatically) oriented material as the basic means by which the language is tested and working through it without any kind of compromise, is something which the self of the learner can recall from experiences in school, experiences which, in our findings, were without exception judged as negative, and rejected.

Nor is there any resulting corrective effect on the development of the identity, even if situation-specific idiom is offered within the respective curriculum, as long as the corresponding speaking strategies continue to be disregarded. All this gives rise not so much to inhibitions on particular points, but to more general constraints, which in turn reactivate (old) fears and inhibitions. Moreover, failure to tackle these difficulties, which are psychological in origin, and which have an inhibiting effect on learning, prevents the achievement of a certain detachment towards the self, and thus also of any increase in self-confidence. If an individual does not know his own «grammar of living and learning», that is, if he is not aware of his learning history, conditioned as it is by the socialisation process, or of the associations within it, moulded by his experiences in the realm of daily life, then his opportunities as far as the assessment of foreign language competence is concerned will remain restricted to the mere linguistic aspects of a foreign language.

This report brings to a close, without the drawing up of any concrete models, the discussion on the potential and limitations of testing strategies for the development of learner-centred tests. The presentation of the results - whether singly or in synopsis - contains those pointers which may be of help in fostering (through assessment processes) the capacity to act authentically in the foreign language. However, they are not to be thought through and put into curricular practice only where it is a question of improving testing strategies. They should also serve to secure consideration of supralinguistic elements, such as, for example, reinforcement of the ability to perceive the testing situation itself in its essential character as a process, or the bringing into consideration of disruptive factors of whatever kind, which need not directly have very much at all to do with the obvious teaching objective, but whose causes are to be sought in a biographical context or in connection with day-to-day events. This is why, as far as further developments are concerned, it is still a matter of pursuing those endeavours which will assist the learner to evaluate his own progress from his own point of view, so that he can himself draw further conclusions regarding he learning process. This would lead us to the situation where the questions in the graph on page 41 are all answered by the learner himself. (For the question of self-assessment I refer to Oscarsson 1978 and his relevant section in this collection.)

This is an aim to which the results presented here can make a very considerable contribution if they succeed in calling into question those ways of looking at matters which have arisen out of one-sided experiences, and in converting the insecurity which these have brought about into a flexible attitude. Insights into the way in which opportunities for self-assessment lead to the experiencing of one's own learning progress provide the best basis for encouraging - in both teachers and learners - the flexible attitude which appears to be a prerequisite for the appropriate use of the foreign language in a given situation. They are also the best way of coping with the insecurities which arise out of the conflict between, on the one hand, attitudes, ideas and strategies which have been hardened by individual life and learning histories, and on the other, new objectives, course content, methods and media.

References

1. A recent opportunity for this was provided by the running of a lavish multi-media programme, the audio-visual product of a group of experts from the Council of Europe, which is aimed at taking increased account of the interests and requirements of adult learners (cf Trim 1977, van Ek 1975). It was broadcast on television under the title «Follow Me», followed up by social modules in the form of courses at adult education institutes.

2. «Just so that I can actually say what it is I'm thinking, so that I can get that across, but without having to stop every second word and think: 'Now how the hell d'you say that, I've gone and forgotten it again ...' That's my problem at any rate ...»

3. Cf Buzan 1978.

4. In essence: Is it my «I» which expresses itself in the foreign language course, or is it the «me», in the sense used by Mead (1968), an identity imposed on me from outside (by, for example, the teaching, the teacher or the language itself)?

5. Cf for example Groeben & Scheele 1977, Black & Butzkamm 1977, Baacke & Schulze 1979, Heinze, Klusemann & Soeffner 1980.

Bibliography

Aus Geschichten lernen. eds. D Baacke, T Schulze. Munich: Juventa, 1979

Berger, P, and T Luckmann: The social construction of reality. New York: Doubleday, 1966.

Black, C., and W. Butzkamm: Klassengespräche - Kommunikativer Unter richt. Heidelberg: Quelle & Meyer, 1977.

Buzan, T: Use your head. London, 1974.

Communication of ideas, ed. L Bryson. New York, 1948.

Edmondson, W, and J House: Let's talk and talk about it. Munich: Urban & Schwarzenberg, 1981.

Ek, J v.: The threshold level. Council of Europe, 1975. Published 1980 as Threshold level English, Pergamon, Oxford.

Groeben, N, and E Scheele: Argumente für eine Psychologie des reflexiven Subjekts. Darmstadt: Steinkopff, 1977.

Interpretationen einer Bildungsgeschichte. eds. T Heinze, H-W Klusemann, and H-G Soeffner. Bensheim: päd. extra, 1980.

Oskarsson, M: Approaches to self-assessment in foreign language learning. Council of Europe, 1978. Published under the same title, Pergamon, Oxford.

Mead, G H: Geist, Identität und Gesellschaft. Frankfurt/M: Suhkramp, 1968.

Schratz, M et al: <u>Lehren und Lernen im Englischunterricht mit Erwachsenen.
Interaktion und Kommunikation im Unterrichts-prozess.</u> Vienna:
Verband Wiener Volksbildung, 1983.

Trim, J L M: <u>Some possible lines of development of an overall structure for
a European unit/credit system for modern language learning by adults.</u>
Strasbourg: Council of Europe, 1977. Published 1980 under the same title,
Pergamon, Oxford.

I.4 SELF-ASSESSMENT OF COMMUNICATIVE PROFICIENCY

by Mats OSKARSSON
Gothenburg University, Sweden

Contents

1.   Introduction

2.   Why self-assessment?

3.   Self-assessment techniques and materials

   3.1 Progress cards and forms

   3.2 Questionnaires, rating scales, check-lists

   3.3 Diaries and log books

   3.4 Informal self-assessment

   3.5 Video and audio cassettes

   3.6 Computer-assisted assessment

References

Appendix: A proposed form for continuous self-assment

1. Introduction

Seen from the learner's point of view foreign language skills may be assessed along two fundamentally different lines. They involve:

a. Assessment in the form of self-report or self-assessment, that is, assessment seen from the learner's own perspective; assessment seen as an internal or self-directed activity;

b. Assessment in the form of examinations (including grading) or administration of tests, that is, assessment seen from the perspective of an «outside agent», typically a teacher or trained examiner; assessment seen as an external or «other directed» activity.

In this section of the report we will be dealing with the former of these two approaches to assessment. In view of the fact that the development of materials and methodologies does not seem to have kept abreast of recent thinking and debate in the area, we will focus our attention on the practical aspects of the subject. We will, thus, concentrate on the discussion and demonstration of some possible concrete techniques for implementing the concept of the learner as an active participant in evaluation matters. We would like to stress that the illustrations chosen represent possible ways of dealing with the question of self-assessment in language learning, not necessarily ideal ways of dealing with it. There is indeed wide scope for developments in this domain of assessment and what we can offer here, for consideration, are merely some modest ideas in rough outline.

2. Why self-assessment?

Assessment according to strategy (b) above is usually considered the only sensible and reliable way of determining someone's proficiency in a foreign language, whereas strategy (a), although it has attracted increasing attention in recent years, is often regarded as quite inappropriate for purposes of assessment, mainly because of its subjective nature. We will argue here, very briefly, that the question of subjectivity does not necessarily invalidate the practice of self-assessment techniques in language testing and evaluation and, furthermore, that self-assessment may be motivated for reasons that go beyond mere evaluation. Our discussion relates primarily to such assessment as has bearing on the language learning situation, in an organised form or as a self-managed activity, and not, for instance, to assessment undertaken for purposes of selection, grading, and accreditation. (Self-assessment as a second-language placement instrument is, however, a real possibility, at least at college or university level, as has been convincingly demonstrated by Le Blanc and Painchaud, 1985.) We fully recognise, furthermore, that the extent to which self-assessment principles may be applied varies a great deal in different educational contexts. What we are trying to do here is to afford a general basis for the discussion and no more.

The notion that the learner's own assessments of acquired skills are inherently unreliable seems to be gainsaid by the growing body of research data in this relatively new field of language testing. The work that has been carried out, often in the form of correlational studies, suggests that the validity of learner judgements is in fact usually fairly high and normally not dramatically lower than that of more established objective criteria such as recognised test results and experienced teachers' estimates (see for instance Raasch, 1979, Evers, 1981, and von Elek, 1982; for a review of the literature, see Oskarsson, 1984). Particularly in cases where the learner has been given relevant training in self-observation and assessment, under proper guidance, the results have been quite encouraging (for a penetrating study of how secondary school students may be brought to an efficient realisation of their grades, by self-assessment, see Huttonen, 1986). The self-assessment approach should therefore be looked upon as a resourceful complement to already existing techniques for measuring language proficiency.

Incorporating self-directed evaluation procedures in language testing may furthermore be justified on the grounds that they are likely to make for widened perspectives, in a general sense, basically because they lead learners as well as teachers to regard assessment as a mutual responsibility, not as the sole responsibility of the teacher. As learners and teachers frequently see things differently - and establish different priorities - shared responsibility is likely to result in changes of emphasis taking place (possibly leading to a boost in communicative skills, for example). Thus shared responsibility for evaluation is, in effect, also conducive to the democratic development of language teaching. This is very natural and appropriate also in view of the fact that assessment should ideally be firmly based on proper needs analysis undertaken in close and active co-operation with learners. Further justification is provided by the fact that assessment is enriched if it can encompass so-called affective aspects of the learning experience (relating, for example, to the learner's willingness or courage to use the language) in addition to such more easily measured cognitive and «performative» variables as mastery of the structure of the language and ability to produce written or spoken language within certain predetermined subject areas. In both of these domains, ie needs analysis and apperception of affective development, the learners themselves must be granted very special insight and they may therefore be expected to be able to make significant contributions to the evaluation.

Briefly, the rationale of self-assessment procedures in language learning may be summed up under the following points (which are, admittedly, somewhat speculative and should therefore be seen, essentially, as a set of propositions which could perhaps be empirically tested):

2.1 Promotion of learning. Self-assessment gives learners training in evaluation, which, in itself, is beneficial to learning. This aspect of self-assessment has been emphasised by many experts, for instance by Trim (1980), who notes that «The education of the learner to make reliable and valid autonomous judgements on the effectiveness of his communication is a necessary part of the learning process» (p. ix).

2.2 Raised level of awareness. Training in self-assessment - basically asking and answering questions like «What have I been doing recently?» «How well have I done?» «When will I be ready to test?» - stimulates learners into considering course content and assessment principles in a more discerning way than is usually the case (ie when learners leave it to the instructor to decide on the «whats», «hows», and «whens» of assessment and instead focus their attention entirely on the results of their performance in whatever test is being administered to them). Application of self-assessment principles thus fosters important evaluative attitudes in the learner.

2.3 <u>Improved goal-orientation</u>. The practice of self-assessment
further tends to enhance learners' knowledge of the wide variety of possible
goals in most language learning contexts. «Other directed» assessment often
leads the learner to accept, and adjust to, for the most part without much
reflection, such goals as are embodied in the tests and testing techniques
employed. Depending on the nature of such testing, this may or may not be
a desirable state of affairs.

As a result of a raised level of awareness and improved knowledge of
the variability of language learning objectives learners will find themselves
in a better position to exert control over their own learning situation, ie they
are, for instance, more likely to attempt to influence classroom activities
in a direction which serves their felt communicative needs. Thus self-assessment
procedures can contribute, in a very real sense, to the democratisation of the
educational process.

2.4 <u>Expanded range of assessment</u>. In certain respects the learner's
own appreciation of his competence in the language is, for natural reasons,
superior to that of an outside tester, namely in areas of affective
learning (relating to attitudes to the language, among other things).
Learner involvement may therefore bring about broadened perspectives in
language testing.

2.5 <u>Shared assessment burden</u>. Dickinson (forthcoming) points out that
a further positive aspect of learner participation in assessment is the
possibility that it may alleviate the assessment burden on the teacher.
This of course still needs to be empirically verified, but it seems to be a
conceivable possibility. The teacher might thus to some extent be freed for
other important duties, among them evaluation that cannot realistically be
conducted by the learner himself (eg final grading).

2.6 <u>Post-course effects</u>. Finally the potential long-term benefits of
self-assessment skills should not be overlooked. Teaching students how to
carry on learning the language independently after the course concludes is
universally considered an important objective in foreign language instruction
(cf for instance Trim, 1981). A necessary ingredient of this skill is the
ability to monitor and assess the progress being made.

3. <u>Self-assessment techniques and materials</u>

In this section we will look at some practical ways and means of
assessing one's own language skills. We will start by examining some
fairly simple and straightforward materials and activities and finish
by commenting briefly on some of the more sophisticated aids that are now,
in the wake of the «electronic explosion» in modern technology, entering the
educational scene.

3.1 <u>Progress cards and forms</u>

The «pupil progress card» is a simple self-assessment tool which has
been used in many different educational settings, for instance within the
framework of the graded objectives schemes in secondary schools in the
United Kingdom (Clark, 1980; see also Buckby in this publication). The
characteristic approach in the graded objectives movement is to define
series of short-term functional goals and to group these together in graded

blocks at various levels of difficulty. Each group of objectives builds on
the previous one, so that the learner advances according to a carefully
structured sequence of increasingly improved abilities and skills. As part
of the assessment procedure the learner may, for instance, use a personal
test card on which he ticks off (in a Learner column) each language activity
when he is sure he can perform it (eg «Ask the way to well-known places»).
The teacher ticks the Teacher column once the learner proves he has mastered
the activity. In the Lothian region of Scotland specifications of such
activities, or language functions, are combined with a Waystage test set
locally and a summative end-of-stage test (Page, 1985).

   Similar self-assessment devices, some of them also incorporating elements
of peer-evaluation in addition to evaluation by tutor, have been used in
other educational settings (see for instance Heindler, 1980, and Dickinson,
forthcoming). Within the framework of a communicative French language
programme, Blanche (1986) tested a reusable self-appraisal form, trying to
establish the developing accuracy of intermittent self-ratings in relation
to grades awarded by instructors. The overall accuracy was reported to be
«impressive». Incidentally, Blanche also found that the students could not
assess their oral achievement grades as well as their oral proficiency grades.

   The following «Continuous Assessment Card» is a proposal for a slightly
elaborated variety of the type of materials that have been used:

CONTINUOUS ASSESSMENT CARD **Name:** *Peter Anderson*			
Test No.	1	2	3
Type of test and date	*Interview* *21 January*	*Role-playing tasks* *19 February*	*...*
Self assessment	*"I thought I could answer about half of the 10 questions satisfactorily. Weak on pronunciation."*	*"Went very well. But there were a few words and phrases I didn't remember. (Important?)"*	*...*
Test result	*7/10*	*Good*	*...*
Comments (by teacher or learner) ᴹᴼ ⁸⁶	*"Slight underestimation. Pronunciation not too bad." (Teacher)* *"Better than I thought." (Student)*	*"You sounded a bit blunt, perhaps." (Teacher)* *"Must practise polite phrases." (Student)*	*...*

The potential use of the card is in language programmes which include
a number of evaluation sessions at regular intervals, eg in the form of
instructor/learner (or learner/learner) role-play interactions or oral
mini-tests. Provision should be made for regular follow-up activities
(discussion), particularly in cases of conspicuous discrepancy between
learner and instructor ratings. As part of the formative feedback mechanism
the learner keeps his card for reference purposes throughout the course,
ie to be used as an illustrative record of the development of his self-
assessment skills.

A more comprehensive self-evaluation instrument, also intended to be
used for continuous assessment purposes, has been proposed in Oskarsson (1984).
The model (reproduced in the Appendix) is to be adapted both as regards the
language of the instructions which, ideally, should be the learner's mother
tongue, and content, which for obvious reasons must be tailored to suit
relevant course objectives and individual learner requirements.

3.2 Questionnaires, rating scales, check-lists

Although the most useful application of self-assessment materials and
procedures clearly is in the area of continuous guided evaluation (ie
evaluation of achievement, for formative purposes), there seems to be a place
for self-assessment in contexts of general proficiency testing as well
(cf results reported by Raasch, 1979; Oskarsson, 1980; Painchaud and Le Blanc,
Le Blanc, 1984). The materials that have been used in experiments and
development work in this area have typically consisted of various kinds of
descriptive rating scales and questionnaires aiming at overall assessment
of perceived ability levels. Example (excerpt from Oskarsson, 1980):

SPEAKING

	I speak the language as well as a well-educated native speaker.	5
		4.5
	I speak the language fluently and for the most part correctly. I have a large vocabulary ...	4
	...	
	I do not speak the language at all.	1

The learner ticks the level he finds appropriate according to
his estimate.

The following German example (excerpt from Raasch, 1979) describes
a situation in which knowledge of French is required. The user indicates
his estimated ability to cope with the situation by ticking one out of
four described levels of performance:

...

Sie wollen Ihren französischen Bekannten Geschichten
aus Ihrem Lehrbuch erzählen, die Sie im Kurs durch-
genommen haben. Wie schätzen Sie Ihre Leistungen ein?

Ich erzähle diese Geschichten

a. fliessend, fast ohne Fehler
b. ziemlich fliessend, mit einigen Fehlern
c. stockend und mit Fehlern, aber verständlich.
d. Ich kann mich in dieser Situation kaum ausdrücken.
...

Experiments have shown that materials of this kind may yield quite valid
results, generally speaking, although the individual ability for realistic
appreciation varies a great deal. Training in using the materials seems to be
needed in many cases.

3.3 Diaries and log books

The use of diaries and log books has been proposed as a possible means of
systematising self-assessment procedures. Carver and Dickinson (1981) suggest
that such record keeping procedures should include the following type of
data: «date», «lesson in textbook», «how I performed», «what difficulties
I had», «what I intend to do next». They emphasise that the system must be
designed in such a way that the user finds it easy to operate. Reporting
on experiments at Eurocentre courses, Schärer (1983) evaluated the pros and
cons of record keeping in the form of learners' log books for purposes of
needs analysis and evaluation. He found, for instance, that the student
needs much guidance and help and that «The log-book can have a discouraging
effect on weak students» (p. 113). Schärer also points out certain positive
aspects of the use of the log book (eg «as an aid to the teacher in
monitoring the students' progress», «For certain students it can act as an
aid to self-study» etc).

Further observations about the use of log books and diaries, with
young students, have been made by Dam et al (1984).

3.4 Informal self-assessment

Informally, ie without the support of a printed, mimeographed, or
otherwise produced pedagogical aid, the student may perceive and evaluate
the effects of his learning efforts in a wide variety of ways, from
experiencing a vague feeling of not having quite grasped the essence of a
teacher point just explained by the instructor to being reduced to a state
of utter frustration as a result of a complete breakdown in communication
when trying to explain something to a native speaker. Among the possible
approaches to such informal assessment may be mentioned mutual assessment
by peers and assessment on the basis of authentic use of the language.
The latter, of course, provides the most valid opportunities for self-
assessment. It is, needless to say, in the actual real-life use of the

language that one may ultimately test one's communicative ability and
therefore the learner is always well advised to try to assess his ability
in terms of his use of the language in natural situations, not in terms of
test scores or in terms of his performance in an artificial learning situation.

We will now turn to some more elaborate ways of engaging the student
in self-assessment tasks.

3.5 Video and audio cassettes

Utilising video equipment in order to produce, for instance,
«progress videos» constitutes an example of how the advances in modern
technology can be exploited for self-assessment purposes. The use of
this medium may by way of example, involve work of the following kind:
students are video-recorded – or video-record each other – doing short
role-plays at regular intervals and are then given the opportunity to view
their scenes and to assess their progress over a period of time. The obvious
advantage of this particular technological aid is that it enables the learner
to experience and evaluate the full range of his communicative skills, linguistic
as well as paralinguistic (that is, with regard to «body language» features
such as facial expressions, body gestures, and eye movements). No other aid
can match the video medium in this respect. Particularly interesting is
the use of the videodisc technique whereby the rather cumbersome and time-
consuming problem of rewinding of tapes is eliminated. (Another advantage
of the videodisc over the videotape is superior still-frame display.
Disadvantages are high costs and, as yet, a dearth of suitable courseware.)

At a lower level of technological sophistication one may use the
ordinary audio cassette recorder for similar purposes. Oral practice and
evaluation may for instance be conducted in the following way: shortly after
working on practice units with their instructor, the learners act out and
record a simple interaction in pairs. The instructor comments on the results
and gives the learners time for additional practice. Then they record the
same conversational exchanges again. In the final phase they compare later
recordings with earlier ones and make estimates of their progress. (As with
the video technique there is now also a more versatile disc-based alternative
to the traditional tape recorder, the so-called random-access audio-recorder,
which is used in combination with computer equipment.)

Interesting development work involving the use of videos and audio
cassettes for purposes of self-assessment of oral skills has been undertaken
at Eurocentre Bournemouth (Ferris, 1983, Oskarsson, 1984) and at CRAPEL,
University of Nancy II (Holec, 1980).

3.6 Computer-assisted assessment

The use of computer-assisted language learning (CALL) technologies and
materials for self-assessment purposes holds out a great deal of hope for
further fruitful development of self-evaluated language learning. Initiatives
and experiments seem to branch out in several directions. Many developers of
programmes have used a systems approach to design. A learning hierarchy
is formulated and a diagnostic mechanism is built into the programme so that
either the learner himself, or else the programme, can decide when review is
needed. An example is the self-study package for English grammar marketed

by Langenscheidt. It is based on a programme developed by D Wyatt and features a running review and extension option which may be regulated by the learner on the basis of an automatic record-keeping procedure built into the programme.

A practical demonstration of computer applications in the area of vocabulary learning and measurement is given by Zettersten (1985). Investigating large-scale testing problems Zettersten found that self-assessment with the aid of computer programmes for use with microcomputers (PCs) is both feasible and suitable. The system used (Videotex, or Viewdata) has a testing feature which produces statements indicating each individual student's range of vocabulary. Similar self-tests in grammar, for classroom use under the guidance of a teacher, have been developed and field-tested (ibid).

Other programmes, like Wordstore (cf Jones and Fortescue, 1986), have carried forward, to great effect no doubt, the time-honoured language learning custom of keeping a vocabulary notebook. Basically such programmes allow the learner to successively build up an individually composed list of words, each with a definition, or a mother-tongue translation, and a context sentence. Self-testing may for instance take the form of responding with the appropriate entries (headwords) to randomly selected and displayed definitions, translations, or context sentences (with the entry gapped out).

Combining computer and video technology into so-called interactive video, where the computer basically functions as a surrogate teacher in that it supplies the learner with suitable practice material on the basis of his demonstrated performance level, is another field under rapid development. If and when such systems can be introduced on a large scale learners will be given yet another tool for measuring, at least informally and indirectly, their mastery of the language.

In sum, the fast-growing province of computer-based language learning and testing is likely to open up many new opportunities for the student who wishes to monitor his own learning.

References

Blanche, P (1986). «The DLIFLC Study». The United States Department of
        Defence Language Institute, Foreign Language Center, Monterey,
        California (mimeo)

Coste, D (ed) (1983). Contributions to a renewal of language learning and
        teaching: some current work in Europe. Strasbourg: Council
        of Europe

Dam, L, Karpinska, M, Nipper, A, and Thomsen, H (1984)
        Autonomi i fremmedsprogstilegnelsen Greve kommune, Denmark
        (mimeo)

Davies, N (1985). «Getting started with microcomputers - a practical
        beginner's guide». System, 13, 2, pp. 119-132

Dickinson, L (forthcoming). Self-Instruction in Language Learning.
        Cambridge: Cambridge University Press

Clark, J (1980). «Lothian region's project on graded levels of achievement
        in foreign-language learning: from principles to practice».
        Modern Languages in Scotland, 19, pp. 61-74

Ferris, D (1983). «The influence of the continuous self-evaluation of
        oral skills on language learning methodology». In D Coste (1983)

Holec, H (1980). Autonomy and foreign language learning. Strasbourg:
        Council of Europe. Published 1981 under the same title,
        Pergamon, Oxford

Huttonen, I (1986). Towards Learner Autonomy in Foreign Language Learning
        in Senior Secondary School. Academic Dissertion, University of
        Oulu, Finland

Jones, C and Fortescue, S (1986). Using Computers in the Language Classroom:
        A Practical Guide for Teachers. London: Longman

Le Blanc, R and Painchaud, G (1985). «Self-Assessment as a Second-Language
        Placement Instrument». TESOL Quarterly, 19, 4, pp. 673-686

Lee, Y P et al (ed. 1985), New Directions in Language Testing. Oxford:
        Pergamon Press

Oskarsson, M (1978). Approaches to Self-Assessment in Foreign Language
        Learning. Council of Europe, Published 1980 under the same
        title, Pergamon, Oxford

Oskarsson, M (1984). Self-Assessment of Foreign Language Skills: A Survey
        of Research and Development Work. Strasbourg: Council of Europe.

Page, B (1985). «Graded objectives in modern language learning».
In Kinsella, V (ed.), Cambridge Language Teaching Surveys 3.
Cambridge: Cambridge University Press

Painchaud, G and Le Blanc, R (1984). «L'auto-évaluation en contexte
scholaire». Etudes de Linguistique Appliquée, 56, Octobre-
Décembre, pp. 88-98

Richterich, R (ed), 1983. Case Studies in Identifying Language Needs.
Pergamon, Oxford

Schärer, R (1983). «Identification of learner needs at Euro-centres».
In Richterich (1983)

Trim, J L M (1980). Foreword in Oskarsson (1980)

Trim, J (1981). Résumé (of Project Report). In Modern Languages 1971-1981
(presented by CDCC Project Group 4). Strasbourg: Council of Europe

Zettersten, A (1985). «Experiments in Large-scale Vocabulary Testing».
In Lee (ed., 1985)

A P P E N D I X

A proposed form for CONTINUOUS SELF-ASSESSMENT

This is a draft form that can be used as a basis for continuous assessment of the progress of learning in a language course. If used as a model the questions ought to be translated into the learners' native language (unless the learners are at an advanced stage). The "test items" ought to be sampled, rephrased, rearranged and supplemented in such a way that they give the learners an opportunity to reflect upon all the various aspects of the course in each individual case.

1. In the last few lessons (days, weeks) we/I have studied/ practised/worked on ...

Fill in the empty spaces with topics and areas of study that are relevant in your case, for example:

(a) ....
(b) ....
(c) ....
(d) ....
(e) ....
(f) ....

        (a) pronunciation of words containing the sound /θ/
        (b) how to greet people
        (c) questions with do/does

Leave out vocabulary ("new words") here, since this is more conveniently dealt with under item 4, below.

2. How well do you master the above topics according to your own estimate?

	not at all	to some extent	fairly well	very well	completely
(a)	☐	☐	☐	☐	☐
(b)	☐	☐	☐	☐	☐
(c)	☐	☐	☐	☐	☐
(d)	☐	☐	☐	☐	☐
(e)	☐	☐	☐	☐	☐
(f)	☐	☐	☐	☐	☐

3. On reflection, to what extent do you find the above topics important in relation to your own personal needs?

	not at all important	not very important	quite important	very important	extremely important
(a)	☐	☐	☐	☐	☐
(b)	☐	☐	☐	☐	☐
(c)	☐	☐	☐	☐	☐
(d)	☐	☐	☐	☐	☐
(e)	☐	☐	☐	☐	☐
(f)	☐	☐	☐	☐	☐

4. We/I have also studied new words of the following type, or within the following subject area(s):

(Put down your native language equivalents if you find it easier.)

(a) ....
(b) ....
(c) ....
(d) ....

5. How well do you know the above vocabulary (areas) according to your own estimate?

	not at all	to some extent	fairly well	very well	completely
(a)	☐	☐	☐	☐	☐
(b)	☐	☐	☐	☐	☐
(c)	☐	☐	☐	☐	☐
(d)	☐	☐	☐	☐	☐

6. On reflection, to what extent do you find the above type of vocabulary (areas) important in relation to your own personal needs?

	not at all important	not very important	quite important	very important	extremely important
(a)	☐	☐	☐	☐	☐
(b)	☐	☐	☐	☐	☐
(c)	☐	☐	☐	☐	☐
(d)	☐	☐	☐	☐	☐

7. Summarizing the last few lessons (days, weeks) I feel I have learnt ...

nothing at all   very little   a little   a good deal   a lot

☐   ☐   ☐   ☐   ☐

8. Looking back, I realise that I ought to change my study habits/ learning style/priorities in the following way:

....

....

....

....

....

9. I judge my weak points to be the following:

....

....

....

....

10. I would want to see instruction in the next few lessons (days, weeks) focused on the following teaching points/skills areas:

....

....

....

....

Follow-up

Discuss your assessment and your points of view with a fellow student or in a small group -- or with your teacher. Try to find out whether others think you tend to overestimate or underestimate your ability and acquired skills and then decide whether you ought to reconsider and readjust your "yardstick". Compare your subjective impressions with other criteria such as test scores, your teacher's evaluation, estimates by your fellow students.

MO 1984

CHAPTER II: SOME NATIONAL DEVELOPMENTS

II.1   GRADED OBJECTIVES IN RELATION TO COMMUNICATIVE

TESTING AND NATIONAL EXAMINATIONS

_____

by Michael BUCKBY,
Language Teaching Centre,
University of York, United Kingdom

_____

1.   The background

In 1986, some 400,000 pupils in schools are taking a test based on
graded objectives for modern languages (GOML). In England, Northern Ireland,
Scotland and Wales there are approximately 90 groups of teachers working on
GOML, each group being independent. Some groups have chosen not to develop
their own objectives and tests, but rather to use those produced by other
groups. There are some 80 syllabuses in existence for the range of
languages currently covered: Chinese, Dutch, French, German, Italian,
Japanese, Russian, Spanish, Swedish, Welsh. The groups are kept in touch
with each other through the Centre for Information on Language Teaching
and Research (CILT). It services a national co-ordinating committee which
organises an annual conference to which all the groups are invited, helps
to organise workshops in France and Germany and the dissemination of the
ideas and materials developed, with the generous help of the French
Government and the Goethe Institut, and produces a regular newsletter which
is sent to every group.

The GOML movement started some ten years ago, with the setting up of
groups in Oxfordshire and York. The main aims were to improve the quality
and to increase the quantity of foreign language learning in British schools.
It is possible in the British educational system to choose to give up the
study of a foreign language at the age of 14, and some 70% of pupils did so.
Of the remaining 30%, the large majority abandoned all foreign language
learning at the age of 16.

There are signs that both of these aims have, to some extent at least,
been reached. On the question of the number of pupils who choose to continue
with foreign language learning, there is a good deal of evidence to support
the notion that GOML have led to a market increase, at least until the age
of 16. There is no firm evidence that similar improvements have been
brought about in the quality of learning, and more research is needed here,
but HMI reports and the subjective impressions of teachers, as expressed
for example at the annual conference, suggest that these improvements are
taking place.

2.   Syllabuses and tests

All the syllabuses and tests have aimed to be communicative, though
there is, of course, considerable difference of opinion about what that
actually means. Although the 80 syllabuses in existence have been produced

at different times and by different groups, they all attempt to reflect the needs, wishes and resources of the learners, to give teachers and learners a clear idea of the testing objectives and to offer a series of objectives which are, at each level, attainable and realistic, as well as being worthwhile in their own right and not merely a preparation for a higher level.

Syllabuses and tests vary in their philosophy, sophistication, degree of definition,number and height of the levels and the extent to which they are communicative. It is, therefore, difficult to generalise about them. However, they do seem to fall roughly into one of two main categories. Those in Category 1 (exemplified by levels 1 to 3 of Oxfordshire and York) were the earliest. They were based on lists of situations which were, in some cases, accompanied by lists of phrases, vocabulary and grammar linked to these situations. They were largely successful in persuading large numbers of teachers to move away from traditional approaches, often hesitantly, to take the first step towards a communicative approach. Produced before the work of the Council of Europe became widely known, with few or no resources and with very little previous work to help, these early syllabuses and tests were intended primarily to present goals simply and effectively, to preserve the freedom of teachers and learners to go beyond the testing goals and to offer tests which could be produced cheaply and administered easily while giving reliable results.

They offered tests of listening, reading and speaking, with no tests of writing. An attempt was made in some groups (eg Oxfordshire) to increase face validity by grouping the listening and reading tests together, linking the various items with a story line. This has been developed since in tests like those of Cambridgeshire, which consist of a number of simulations which include a variety of spoken, reading and writing activities within one overall task. Examples of Category 1 tests follow:

Listening (York level 1): the pupils listen to short, scripted recordings made by native speakers, and try to answer these questions, in English.

1. Listen to find out how much the oranges cost.
    They cost:

    a. 3F 20
    b. 3F 30
    c. 4F 40
    d. 4F 50

2. Listen to find out what the shopkeeper asks the customer.
    He asks:

    a. How much cheese the customer wants
    b. What sort of cheese the customer wants
    c. How many boxes she wants
    d. If she wants anything else

3. Listen to find out what the shopper wants.
    She wants:

    a. Four stamps
    b. Three stamps
    c. Four postcards
    d. Four postcards and four stamps

4. Listen to find out how much the shopper is charged.
    How much does she pay?

Reading (York level 3): the pupils read short texts (signs, notices, etc)
and answer questions in English, eg

1. In a camp guide you see CAMPING OUVERT A PARTIR DU PREMIER JUIN
    What does this mean?

    a. The camp-site is open until 1 June
    b. The camp-site is closed in June
    c. The camp-site opens on 1 June
    d. This is a first-class camp-site

2. You are in Paris, looking for an underground station.
    What sign do you look for?

    a. Gare St. Lazare
    b. Métro
    c. Arrêt d'autobus
    d. Tête de station

3. You see the sign SOLDES in the window of a big store.
    What does it mean?

    a. There is a sale on
    b. Everything in the window is sold
    c. The shop has been sold
    d. The shop is for sale

The test also presents longer texts, again with questions in English, to be
answered in English, eg:

Part Two

Read this letter written by a French boy to his English penfriend and then try to answer all the questions.

Cher Ami,

Tu me poses des questions sur mon village. C'est un petit village sur la côte de la Bretagne. Son industrie principale est la pêche.

Je vais à une nouvelle école qui est près du port. Je n'aime pas beaucoup l'école et ma matière préférée, ce sont les travaux manuels. J'aime ça parce que c'est un cours pratique. Le mois dernier, par exemple, nous avons commencé à faire un petit bateau et la semaine dernière nous l'avons fini. Ce weekend, avec des camarades, j'ai essayé notre bateau sur la mer. C'était formidable! Il n'y a pas eu un seul problème.

Comme tu le sais déjà, mon père et mes deux frères sont pêcheurs. Moi aussi, plus tard, je voudrais être pêcheur. C'est un métier assez dangereux, mais je pense que c'est une vie intéressante. Qu'est-ce que tu veux faire plus tard dans la vie?

Dans ta réponse, parle-moi de l'école où tu vas et de tes ambitions.

Amicalement,
Jean

1 Where is Jean's village?
a) On the British coast
b) Near a small fishing port
c On the coast of Brittany
d Near an industrial town in Brittany

2 Where has Jean made his boat?
a) At the port
b) On the sea
c) At home
d) At school

3 Which members of Jean's family are already fisherm

_____

4 According to Jean, what is the advantage of being a fisherman?

_____

And what is the disadvantage?

_____

5 What two things does Jean ask his penfriend to wri him about?

_____

Speaking (Oxfordshire level 2): pupils are required to take part in role-playing tasks, with English instructions, eg

At the station

a. Ask for a single ticket to Neuville.
b. Ask if you have to change.
c. Ask where the waiting room is.

The pupils are also asked some questions in French, designed to provoke an interactive exchange, eg

a. Qu'est-ce que ton père/ta mère fait dans la vie?
b. Combien de frères et de soeurs as-tu?
c. Quels sont tes passetemps?
d. Quelles matières préfères-tu à l'école?

The syllabuses and tests which fall into Category 2 (exemplified by those produced in West Sussex, Lothian and level 5 from York) were developed later, with more time, research, resources and access to other work, and especially work produced and inspired by the Council of Europe. These syllabuses are much longer and more detailed than those in Category 1. They are also more sophisticated, drawing attention to more of the elements which contribute to effective communication (eg awareness of social and psychological roles, communication strategies). They put an increased emphasis on the use of authentic texts and tasks, including mixed-skills tasks. Some examples follow.

<u>Listening</u> (York level 5): the pupils listen to unscripted recordings made by native speakers and answer the questions in English.

A French teacher who has stayed at your house during a school exchange rings up to ask your help in finding some lost property.

a Where was the article probably left?

_____

b You are shown the following items of lost property. Which is the article described?

A   B   C   D

☐   ☐   ☐   ☐

Tick the correct box.

c Where are you asked to send it if you find it?

_____

You are driving in Paris and you hear this commercial on the car radio. The people you are with do not understand French well, and miss the details but they hear the name of Rod Stewart. Give the following information about the commercial in English:

1. Give the date of Rod Stewart's concert
2. Give the time at which it starts.

Some research has been carried out into the use of video for testing listening comprehension at this level.

Reading (York level 5)

The owner of a local «Bed and Breakfast» came across this brochure whilst on holiday in France. He is interested in seeing how his business might become involved in such a scheme. He wants to check his understanding of some of the details with you. These are the questions he has. Read the brochure and write down the answers.

a. What three features of York does the advertisement mention to attract tourists?

i. _____
ii. _____
iii. _____

b. How much extra would the holiday cost (in francs) for an adult wanting a single room?

_____

c. What does the holiday price include?

i. Number of nights in the hotel?

_____

ii. Which meals are provided?

_____

ESCAPADE A YORK PENDANT 3 JOURS.

York vous étonnera, notamment avec ses maisons anciennes, son immense cathédrale et son célèbre musée du chemin de fer.

Notre formule comprend :
. Le voyage "bateau + train" aller-retour de Calais, Boulogne ou Dunkerque jusqu'à York (via Londres).
. L'hébergement en demi-pension (petits déjeuners + dîners) au "Friars Garden Hotel" (situé dans la gare de York), pour 2 nuits. Embarquement conseillé avant midi pour une arrivée à York avant le dîner.

Le "York Minster" à York.

Prix en chambre double et par personne	
● adulte:	1.090,00 F
● enfant:	850,00 F
● supplément chambre individuelle	70,00 F

Speaking (York level 5): in addition to taking part in a real
conversation with the examiner, the pupils are required to take
part in a role creation task, eg:

1.   While on visit to Dijon, you have lost your wallet
        or purse. You think you lost it yesterday, on a number
        105 bus. You go to the lost property office to see if
        it has been found. Your teacher will play the part of
        the clerk.

2.   You are looking for a hotel room in Boulogne. You go to
        the syndicat d'initiative. Try to get the information
        below and write the information you are given on the
        answer sheet provided. Write the information in English.

        1.   Is there a hotel with a room free?
                If so, what is the name of the hotel?

        2.   How much is it per night for a room with a shower?

        3.   Is breakfast included? If not, how much is it?

        4.   How do you get to this hotel?

Writing (York level 5): your French penfriend has sent you this letter.
Write a reply to it, in French, on page x.

Answer your friend's questions and describe what you did last Saturday
evening. Let her know if she will be able to come and stay with you
in the holidays and, if so, when and what you will do together. If it
is not possible for her to stay with you, explain why.

Write between 115 and 130 words in French, excluding your address and
the date.

Sèvres, le 2.4.1985

Salut,

J'espère que tu vas bien ainsi que ton frère et ta famille.

Je te remercie beaucoup pour le cadeau que tu m'as envoyé il m'a beaucoup plu, car vois-tu, cela faisait plus d'une semaine que je voulais acheter le livre de Marilyn Monroe et le poster que tu m'as envoyés.

Pour mon anniversaire, mes parents m'ont autorisé à faire une boum samedi soir avec plusieurs amis. On a installé la vidéo et préparé un buffet. On s'est bien amusé pendant toute la soirée, on a écouté des disques, dansé...

Et toi, comment vas-tu ? Quel temps fait-il en Angleterre ?

J'aimerais venir te voir pendant les grandes vacances. Notre école organise des voyages pour aller en Angleterre et j'en profiterais pour te voir, et en même temps pour visiter ton pays qui est bien beau.

Je te quitte en espérant que tu me répondras rapidement.

Amitiés

Dominique.

Within this second category, there has been some development recently from an emphasis on a functional-notional approach, with a tendency towards pre-determined outcomes to learning, towards an emphasis on a purposeful communicative approach, which leaves more scope for pupils' autonomy and initiatives in learning and testing.

In both categories, the learners' L1 (English) is used regularly in the tests to perform certain tasks. Questions and answers on reading and listening texts are largely in the L1, as are the instructions for the speaking and writing tasks. This does not necessarily imply that English is used in these ways in the teaching and learning process. Its use in the tests is justified on four main counts:

i.   To increase the validity of the reading and listening tests, by enabling learners to demonstrate to the maximum their capacity for reading and listening with understanding. They are not prevented from showing their understanding of worthwhile texts, either by a failure to understand the questions or to compose an answer in the foreign language. As they are, the tests are more valid tests of listening and reading.

ii.   This use of English is seen to represent the use of the foreign language in real life, outside the classroom, in an authentic way. For example, one is more likely to be called upon to summarise, or to answer questions on, a text for someone who is not able to understand the text, because they do not understand the language. Had they understood the text, they would not need to ask questions about it. For the same reason that they cannot understand the text, they are unlikely to ask questions in the foreign language, or to understand answers in that language.

Similarly, it is considered that learners at this level are likely to prepare for a foreign language encounter by thinking, in their L1, along such lines as: «I need to buy a return ticket to Sèvres ... What should I say?» This is seen as more likely than such processes taking place in the L2.

iii. One role which the learners are expected to master is the ability to interpret between monolinguals in the two languages.

iv.   More technically, and perhaps less importantly, questions and instructions in the L2 create testing problems. Questions tend to give away much of the L2 which they are trying to test, and this can lead to all sorts of examiners' tricks which frequently confuse learners in ways which are quite irrelevant to the skills and competences which the test aims to test.

3.   National examinations

This is a period of great change in public examinations in the United Kingdom. There has been a strong move towards centralised control over syllabuses and examinations. Examinations at 16+ and 18+ exert a very strong influence on the teaching in secondary schools. In the case of foreign languages, the new national criteria and the syllabuses, and examinations based on them, have been shaped to a large extent by GOML. The new defined syllabuses and examinations, due to be introduced in 1988, are likely, in their turn, to strengthen greatly the move towards GOML, communicative language learning and the view that the large majority of pupils in school should enjoy successful foreign language learning.

The GCSE (in England, Northern Ireland and Wales) and Standard Grade (in Scotland) share many of the important aims of GOML. These include:

- an emphasis on the importance of practical communication skills;

- the use of authentic texts and tasks;

- a move away from an emphasis on norm-referencing towards criterion-referencing;

- the importance of having clearly defined aims and objectives which attempt to reflect the needs, interests and resources of the learners.

However, many of the shortcomings of traditional examining as regards assessment and the reporting of results remain. The draft proposals for grade criteria for the GCSE, which are currently being discussed, represent an attempt to overcome these shortcomings. The proposals aim primarily to produce a system which:

- encourages and rewards mastery of specified competences;

- makes all grades awarded a positive statement, showing what candidates did successfully;

- makes the meaning of all grades clear to consumers (eg learners, teachers and employers).

In the model proposed by the National Criteria, all candidates have to enter for the common core (shaded in the grid below) and are left free to decide which additional elements to enter for:

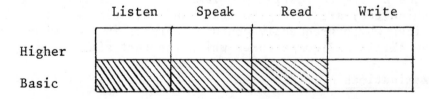

The Grade Criteria maintain this approach and the four domains of listening, speaking, reading and writing. To bring each domain into line with the seven overall grades to be awarded (A-G), seven Areas of Competence (AoC) are defined within each domain, with four at Basic and three at the Higher level (which accounts primarily for three grades, A-C). This produces a rather more detailed grid for the setting and assessing of exams:

		Listen	Speak	Read	Write
Higher	7				
	6				
	5				
Basic	4	///	///	///	
	3	///	///	///	
	2	///	///	///	
	1	///	///	///	

Within each AoC, the required competences are clearly defined, in terms of the social and psychological roles, topics, settings, tasks and levels of attainment. For each AoC in which a candidate shows mastery, by completing satisfactorily 70% or more of the tasks set, one point would be awarded. The overall grade would be determined by the number of points gained:

Grade	Points
A	24-28
B	21-23
C	18-20
D	14-17
E	9-13
F	4-8
G	1-3

A candidate would be awarded a grade and given a profile showing how the points had been awarded, eg

	1	2	3	4	5	6	7
L	1	1	1				
S	1	1					
R	1	1					
W							

(This candidate has seven points and thus grade F)

The grid below summarises the seven AoC for listening, as an illustration of the demands being made:

BASIC LEVEL			
RESTRICTED RANGE (8 topics and settings)		FULL BASIC RANGE (10-12 topics and settings)	
AREA OF COMPETENCE 1	AREA OF COMPETENCE 2	AREA OF COMPETENCE 3	AREA OF COMPETENCE 4
... listen to and understand important points and details in short instructions, announcements and requests in French.	... listen to and understand specific details in short dialogues in French.	... listen to and understand important points and details in instructions, announcements and requests in French.	... listen to and understand specific details in interviews and monologues (e.g. weather forecasts) in French.

Candidates are able to ...

HIGHER LEVEL		
TOTAL RANGE (approx. 14 topics and settings)		
AREA OF COMPETENCE 5	AREA OF COMPETENCE 6	AREA OF COMPETENCE 7
... identify themes and details in announcements, instructions, requests, interviews and dialogues in French.	... identify themes and details (including attitudes, ideas and emotions) in announcements, instructions, requests, interviews and dialogues in French.	... draw conclusions from and see relations within extended announcements, instructions, requests, interviews and dialogues in French.

The criteria for assessment in the new examinations will clearly reflect those of GOML. They emphasise giving positive rewards for effective communication, and aim to enable candidates to gain credit for what they know and can do. Another important principle is that the criteria for assessment are freely available to all teachers and learners. This example of the criteria for assessing the conversation part of a Basic-level oral examination comes from the NEA French syllabus for 1988:

«Conversation

The candidate's performance in the conversation will be assessed according to the effectiveness of communication with a sympathetic native speaker. The following criteria will be used, each weighted equally:

Pronunciation: the extent to which accent, intonation and stress facilitate (or interfere with) effective communication.

Accuracy: the extent to which grammatical accuracy facilitates (or interferes with) effective communication.

Fluency: the extent to which readiness of response and continuity of performance contribute to effective communication.

Independence: the extent to which the candidate is able to initiate conversation and/or to expand on bare essentials to make an independent contribution to the conversation.

Content: the amount of relevant information which the candidate is able to convey in relation to the topics for the conversation.

In each of the above categories, the candidate will be awarded 0, 1 or 2 marks according to the level of performance as indicated below provided that the conversation is relevant to the given topics. Largely irrelevant conversations will not be marked according to these criteria. The examiners will, under these circumstances, decide on what, if any, credit can be given for the performance as a whole.

Pronunciation

0   Pronunciation is such that the message would be unintelligible to a sympathetic native speaker.

1   In spite of causing some difficulty for immediate comprehension or leading to some initial misunderstanding, pronunciation is such that the overall message is intelligible to a sympathetic native speaker, allowing for requests for repetition or clarification.

2   Although requiring an effort of concentration from a sympathetic native listener, the message is for the most part intelligible, causing only occasional difficulty.

Accuracy

0   The frequency and/or type of errors made are a permanent barrier to communication

1   In spite of causing some difficult for immediate comprehension or leading to some initial misunderstanding, the overall message is intelligible to a sympathetic native speaker, allowing for requests for repetition or clarification.

2   Although requiring an effort of concentration from a sympathetic native speaker, the message is for the most part intelligible, causing only occasional difficulty.

Fluency

0   The candidate does not respond readily. Delivery is slow, halting and disjointed to the extent that communication is seriously impaired.

1   Although the candidate may be slow to respond and delivery may
     be hesitant in places, there is some continuity of performance
     allowing a reasonable exchange of information to take place.

2   Readiness of response and continuity of performance is such
     that the exchange of information has a reasonable flow in spite
     of pauses.

Independence

0   The candidate makes no independent contribution to the conversation.

1   Although the candidate is dependent on the initiative of the native
     speaker and relies largely on information supplied in order to
     respond, the candidate is able to use the information appropriately
     for his/her own purposes.

2   Although largely dependent on the initiative of the tolerant
     native speaker, shows some ability to expand on minimal replies

Content

0   Coverage of the topics inadequate. Hardly any relevant information
     conveyed to the native speaker.

1   Although coverage of the topics is limited, some relevant information
     is conveyed.

2   The candidate is able to convey relevant information on most of the
     aspects covered in the conversation.»

The system proposed for Grade Criteria would have implications for the
teaching and for the ways candidates should be entered for the GCSE, the main
ones of which are:

-    it would strengthen the notion of mastery (developed in the Graded
     Objectives movement) and would lead to teachers discovering and
     concentrating on what learners can do well and enjoy doing;

-    pupils would be entered for elements of the whole exam at which they
     were likely to succeed. Since no «booby prizes» are available for
     picking up a few marks here and there, candidates could be disadvantaged
     by being entered for everything, unless they are likely to score 70%
     or more: less advanced learners would waste learning and examining
     time by trying to have a go at everything, and would be much more
     likely to achieve their best by concentrating, in the learning and
     the exam, on what they are capable of doing really well.

4.   Areas of research

The rapid progress made in recent years has been exhilarating, but the
need for thorough research is urgent in order properly to evaluate and consolidate
this progress. Some of the most important needs in terms of research and
development work are:

- to show that a GOML approach does produce better learning than traditional approaches;

- to develop clear criteria for the grading of texts and tasks;

- to develop techniques of validly and reliably assessing performance in a criterion-referenced way;

- to renew the GOML produced ten years ago;

- to produce clearer guidelines about what constitutes authentic texts and tasks for learning and testing;

- to investigate the place of grammar in a communicative approach;

- to develop guidelines for the teaching and learning of understanding and producing discourse;

- to investigate the development of appropriate communication strategies at school level.

5. Selective bibliography

OMLAC. New objectives in modern language teaching. Hodder and Stoughton, 1977.

Graded French tests (Levels 1-3). Nelson, 1980.

Buckby, M et al. Graded objectives and tests for modern languages: an evaluation. CILT, 1981.

HM Inspectors. The use of graded tests of defined objectives and their effect on the teaching and learning of modern languages in the County of Oxfordshire. DES, 1982.

Page, B. «Graded objectives in modern language learning». Language teaching and linguistics, October 1983.

Dunning, R (ed). French for communication. University of Leicester, 1983.

Clark and Hamilton. Syllabus Guidelines 1: communication. CILT, 1984.

HM Inspectorate. Classroom practice in schools in north-west England: preparing pupils for graded tests of defined objectives in modern languages. DES, 1985.

Buckby, M. «The use of English in the foreign language classroom», in York Papers in Language Teaching (ed. P S Green). University of York, 1985.

GCSE: The National Criteria (French). DES, HMSO, 1985.

Draft Grade Criteria (French).   Secondary Examinations Council, 1985.

Buckby and Howson.   The use of video-taped material in the testing of
    listening comprehension of French at 16+.   LTC, University of York, 1985.

French syllabus for the 1988 examination, Northern Examining Association,
    1986.

Clark, J.   Curriculum renewal in school foreign language learning.   OUP
    (forthcoming).

II.2 EVALUATION IN THE EDUCATIONAL CONTEXT

by Jane SAMUEL
Institut National de la Recherche Pédagogique
France

Evaluation, if it is to be worthwhile and useful, must take account of several factors. It must be carried out in a context and correspond to the specific objectives defined in the learning of foreign languages. It must be positive and enable the learner to monitor his progress towards achieving these objectives and to judge what level he has reached.

In what context is evaluation in foreign languages carried out?

The context may be that of a school, in which case objectives and content are defined nationally. It is, thus, carried out in a broad context of which foreign languages form a part. This means that the pupil has to prove in an examination that he has reached the level required at a specific stage in the syllabus.

The context may be one of adults with specific needs who seek a qualification in one or more clearly defined fields, comprehension and/or expression for example. In this case, evaluation is, to all intents and purposes, independent.

However, it is possible, in both these cases, to specify requirements corresponding to the levels of competence to be achieved.

The following is an account of the context of schools in France.

1. Objectives:

    These are threefold:

a. studying how the language works through its analytical and explicit practice;

b. using it as a means of communication: the development of skills in the fields of expression and comprehension;

c. learning about the civilisation of countries whose languages are being learnt.

    The three objectives may thus be described as linguistic, communicative and cultural.

2. Content:

    The content to be taught is specified in the various syllabuses on a school year basis and marks a progression in the acquisition of skills. It takes account of the timetable arrangements in schools and permits a harmonisation of standards in public examinations that have been devised at regional level.

The cultural content is not explicitly defined in the case of English, given the scope and diversity of the Anglo-Saxon world, although it is clearly specified for German and Spanish, for example.

A lexical programme is defined for the four years of secondary school corresponding, with a few exceptions, to the content proposed by the Council of Europe in its Threshold Level.

The linguistic content is decided upon for each year in the «college» and «lycée» from the first to the last years. The English syllabus has two components: one is strictly grammatical, covering three major aspects - the sentence, the nominal group and the verbal group; the other is functional and semantico-grammatical concentrating on communication whilst having the same grammatical content. It, too, has three aspects - (a) the functions of language, socialising, suasion, appreciation: judgement, evaluation, information and discussion; (b) modality (the way in which the speaker expresses his point of view or mood); (c) semantico-grammatical categories (notions), ie qualification, quantification, possession, spatial, temporal, aspectorial and logical references. The aim of this twofold presentation is to emphasise the communicative objective without producing mere lists or a kind of phrase book.

3. Evaluation:

Evaluation is carried out on two levels: either for the purposes of the baccalauréat or for the «collège» certificate.

A. The baccalauréat

Evaluation at the baccalauréat level has recently undergone certain changes which, while respecting the aforesaid three objectives, place greater emphasis on the field of communication.

The new tests were devised on the basis of the work and proposals of a working party. They should be further improved with the introduction of a comprehension test for which an oral document will be used in all types of baccalauréat. There are two categories of tests, not so that candidates may have a choice, but depending on the type of baccalauréat they enter for, the modern languages test being compulsory for all (some 400,000 candidates).

Written tests: These aim to evaluate the following three types of competence, each being tested by a series of specific questions:

. Linguistic skills, the idea being to check the candidate's knowledge in this field;

. Reading comprehension: various types of exercises are designed to check the quality of the candidate's comprehension of a written text: general meaning (the gist), overall structure and most obvious key points; understanding of detail, checking of the ideas formulated on first reading and appreciation of the implicit;

. Writing competence: there are two different types of test: one is a semi-guided written test in which candidates are given instructions defining the task assigned and giving hints on how to tackle it; the second is less rigid and requires the candidate to present, defend, discuss and comment on a point of view, thus enabling him to express his own opinions; this permits examiners to assess the richness of his expression and the degree of his language autonomy.

Each part of the test is evaluated separately and has a percentage attached to it which can vary according to the type of baccalauréat. The percentage attributed to «communication» tests, both reading and writing, corresponds, generally, to 70% of the whole. Precise criteria are used in assessing the writing competence. These are as follows:

- The task has been completed: what the candidate has written corresponds to what was requested of him; relating facts, conveying an opinion or information on a subject, refuting an opinion, persuading, backing up; etc. What has been written is intelligible and the grammatical errors in no way obscure the intelligibility of what has been expressed.

So as to appreciate whether the candidate has taken the trouble to structure his discourse, assessment is made of development of a train of thought, clear exposition of ideas or point of view, course of events, internal logic, articulation in development. The candidate is not given free rein but his performance depends essentially on the nature of the task.

- Richness of expression: the quality of the language. Account must be taken of the candidate's ability to use appropriately and for his own ends the sum of what he has learnt. He must demonstrate that he is capable of mobilising his knowledge, of making choices, finding the right word or phrase corresponding to what he wants to express: register, language level, accuracy, nuance.

- Language accuracy: assessment is made of the type of error, the rate of its reoccurrence, its seriousness (is it a major or minor error for a candidate in the last year, and how many errors are made?).

Each criterion can be given a coefficient.

The following are examples of tests for reading comprehension and written expression:

Free expression:

1. The following graffiti were recently seen in New Orleans:

«Emigrants cause unemployment - unemployment causes crime.»

Somebody else had added underneath: «FEAR HATE RACISM».

Explain the meaning of those graffiti and develop the conflicting positions they reflect.

2. You have the possibility of a two-month visit to the USA. Would that visit appeal to you or would you rather visit another country? Give your reasons.

Semi-guided expression:

Write a dialogue between someone in favour of personal computers and someone who is against.

Use phrases such as: I can't stand it; I dislike; I can't bear; to be fond of; to be responsible for; to cause; to blame...for...

Reading comprehension :

The sidewalks were crowded with well-dressed crowds. The sun
stood at their backs and counted the seconds until they got to
work.

How long had Irina been in New York? Arkady asked himself.
Why did she have so few clothes in the closet?

It would be snowing in Moscow. If they had a sun like this
they'd be on the embankment, stripped to the waist, basking like
seals.

The painters were at work again across the way. The clerks on
the next floor would pick up a phone, say no more than a word or
two and set it down. In Moscow an office telephone was an instrument for gossip considerately provided by the state; it was
hardly ever used for work, but it was always busy.

He turned on the television to cover the sound while he worked
on the lock with a hairpin. It was a well-made lock.

Why would painters work with the windows shut?

In the church garden old men in dirty clothes shared a bottle in
slow motion.

The television showed mostly detergents, deodorants and as-
pirin. There were short interviews and dramatic sketches in between.

When Al brought in a ham-and-cheese sandwich and coffee,
Arkady asked him what American writer he liked—Jack London
or Mark Twain? Al shrugged. John Steinbeck or John Reed?
Nathaniel Hawthorne or Ray Bradbury? Well, that's all the ones
I know, Arkady said and Al left.

The offices emptied for lunch. Wherever the sun reached the
sidewalk, someone stopped and ate out of a paper bag. Paper
wrappers floated five or ten stories up between buildings. Arkady
threw the window up and leaned out. The air was cold and smelled
of cigars, exhaust and frying meat.

He saw the same woman in a white-and-black imitation fur
coat go in and out of the hotel with three different men.

Cars were huge and dented and had a plastic gloss. There was
an intense level of noise, of things being hauled and raised and
hammered, as if, just out of sight, the city was being torn down
and the cars were being instantly and carelessly manufactured.

The colors of the cars were ridiculous, as if a child had been
allowed to color them.

How to categorize the men in the church garden? Social para-
sites? A "troika" of drinkers? What did they drink here?

London wrote about the exploitation of Alaska, Twain about
slavery, Steinbeck about economic dislocation, Hawthorne about
religious hysteria Bradbury about interplanetary colonialism,
and Reed about soviet Russia. Well, that's all I know, Arkady
thought.

People carried so many paper bags. Not only did these people
have money, they had things to buy.

He took a shower and dressed in his new clothes. They fit perfectly, felt incredibly fine and made his own shoes immediately
ugly. Nicky and Rurik, he remembered, had Rolex watches.

The clothes bureau had a Bible. Far more surprising was the
telephone book. Arkady tore out the addresses of Jewish and
Ukrainian organizations, folded them and put them inside his
socks.

Black police in brown uniforms directed traffic. White police
in black uniforms wore guns.

Irina had hidden the criminals Kostia Borodin and Valerya
Davidova. She was implicated in the state crimes of smuggling
and sabotage of industry. She knew the Moscow town prosecutor
had been a KGB officer. What was waiting for her in the Soviet
Union?

Cabs were yellow. Birds were gray.

GORKY PARK
Martin Cruz Smith, 1981 Pan Books

Read the text carefully several times.

Then:

- 1.   Choose a suitable title for the text:

  -   A Russian back in Moscow.

  -   An American writer in New York City.

  -   A Russian in New York City.

  -   An American writer in Moscow.

- 2.   Who does «HE» refer to?   (lines 14-32-49-51)

  Who does he talk to?

  Name the person he is thinking of.

- 3.   Is he inside or outside a building?

  Justify your answer with at least three significant elements
  from the text.

- 4.   His vision of the city is: objective, critical, ambiguous,
  ironical, enthusiastic.

  Choose the most appropriate adjectives in the list and justify
  your choice with examples from the text.   (adjectives, adverbs,
  groups of words ...)

- 5.   «People carried so many paper bags. Not only did these people
  have money but they had things to buy.»

  What has he got in the back of his mind when he thinks so?
  Answer in one, two or three words.

  Pick out another passage in the text expressing the same feeling.

Oral tests: Oral tests used to consist of the questioning of the
candidate on a text studied during the school year and chosen by the examiner
from a list submitted by the former. This type of questioning tended to
degenerate into a commentary which was often learned by heart and it was
difficult to determine the candidate's ability to express his own views
and to make any meaningful assessment of his communicative ability.

The test now consists of two parts: the first is still along the lines
of the original form of questioning, that is, on the basis of a text known
to the candidate, and it enables the examiner to check the knowledge acquired
in the field of civilisation and the quality of the candidate's oral
discursive expression. The second consists of a conversation with the
candidate on the basis of an unseen document. The aim here is to enable
examiners to make a more reliable assessment of how far the candidate is
able to hold a spontaneous conversation: intelligibility, richness of
expression, authenticity of the means employed, appropriateness of reactions
to leading comments from the other person, ability to reason and «negotiate»
with him.

The quality of the candidate's performance is evaluated on the basis of the following precise criteria.

Criterion 1: the contract has been fulfilled:

The candidate has taken the initiative in opening the conversation;

he has presented the theme he intended to develop;

he has presented and developed a sufficient number of arguments, facts and reasons for his choice with which to present and justify his point of view, his opinion;

he has responded appropriately to the examiner's comments; reaction to the unexpected, use of gap-fillers, etc.

Criterion 2: phonological quality of the language:

Articulation, delivery, rhythm, intonation, stress.

A variety of five levels could be referred to, eg level (1): the candidate's speech has natural rhythm, is coherent, has (vocalic and consonantic) intonation, stress in the right place (sentence and word); level (5): the candidate's speech is imperfect phonologically, having no diphthongs, no stress, French sounding consonants and vowels and an incoherent system.

Criterion 3: richness of expression: wide range of vocabulary, facility of expression, accuracy in the use of various structures, enabling the candiate to modulate his train of thought. Reference may again be made to several levels, eg level (1): rich and varied use of language and careful expression; level (5): language modelled entirely on French.

Criterion 4: grammatical accuracy:

Level 1: few syntactical errors;

Level 2: a few errors but non-recurring; candidate corrects himself.

Level 3: more errors but the candidate is still able to correct himself;

Level 4: many recurring basic errors, grammatical points frequently overlooked;

Level 5: a great many recurring basic errors, faulty syntax and language entirely modelled on French and at the limit of intelligibility.

Each criterion is given a coefficient.

Two examples are attached of documents given to candidates at the beginning of the test which serve as a point of departure for the conversation. These documents may be drawn from three categories: iconographic documents, short written documents or short oral documents. The candidate is given some ten minutes to observe and analyse the document and to reflect on what he intends to say. (He has the choice between two documents).

Sports Fans

"For Sports Fans, a Season of Discontent" [Analysis, August 30], and a season of waking up to the fact that baseball, football, ice hockey, basketball—as performed by professional players—have very little to do with sport. They rather are part of the entertainment industry, complete with unions, strikes and strike threats and highly overpaid performers, often acting like prima donnas.

O. S. GUTMAN
Southbury, Conn.

The article forgot to look at the word "professional." Is it O.K. for other professions (doctors, lawyers, etc.) to make over $100,000 a year till they're 65 or older? A professional athlete can be injured on any given day, and a career can end right there. If you look at all professions, you will find problems with drugs and alcohol abuse, as they are societal problems. Do people honestly think Elizabeth Taylor is worth 4 million dollars a movie?

LARRY HOCH
Hammond, Ind.

Look carefully at the picture.

Everybody wants to be in LA. Why?

Remarks: The changes in the tests mark a change in direction and reflect the increasing desire to place more emphasis on the communicative function of modern languages. There is, however, still a drawback connected with the very concept of the baccalauréat: the test forms part of a whole and success or failure in the examination depends on the total number of points obtained in all the compulsory tests, a total which must be either greater than or equal to half of the grand total. Each subject has a coefficient which varies according to the type of baccalauréat chosen and, it has to be said, in certain predominantly scientific sectors performance in languages has hardly any bearing on the final result.

For example, the oral language test in baccalauréat C (scientific) has a maximum coefficient of 60 points out of a total of 440. A candidate may very easily pass with a mark of 6/60 in languages, the result being largely offset by good marks in mathematics and physical sciences (200 points overall). Accordingly, motivation is generally low and it is clear that success in the baccalauréat does not automatically mean that the candidate has reached a certain level of competence in foreign languages. The effect of the system of compensation is considerable.

B.   «Collège» certificate (Brevet des Collèges)

This examination is taken at the end of four years of secondary education. It is organised quite differently: there is no specific examination for pupils in state schools, evaluation being carried out on the basis of continuous assessment. The system proposed consists in giving each pupil a mark obtained as follows: the average of the marks obtained by pupils throughout the school year is taken, and to it is added, in some cases, a mark obtained in a test devised by the teachers. The value and meaning of such a system are questionable; the average mark is actually worked out by totalling the marks given throughout the year for very different exercises which correspond to different and non-comparable objectives. What does a mark of 11/20 mean when it is the average obtained by adding up the marks given to pupils for comprehension of an oral and/or written document, for written and/or oral expression, for reciting a text learnt by heart, for reading aloud, etc. What conclusions can be drawn from it? What can such a pupil do? Can he understand instructions? Can he make himself understood? Can he cope with a grammar exercise? No one can say. Furthermore, in view of the importance attached to the mark 10/20 - the fine dividing line between what is acceptable and what is regarded as failure - pupils are very satisfied if they obtain a mark in the region of 10.

In addition, the part that the foreign language plays in the final result is relatively insignificant, the coefficient allocated to it being only 2.

Thus, in the case of both the baccalauréat and the «collège» certificate, it is actually impossible to claim that:

«A person who has passed the baccalauréat is able to ...;
a pupil who has obtained the 'collège' certificate is able to ...»

If we look at the way in which most pupils in schools are assessed throughout the year, it is clear that evaluation does not enable the pupil to form any precise idea of the levels s/he has reached, of what s/he is able to do. Very often evaluation is carried out on a negative basis. For example, the number of errors is counted up, they are given a certain value and subtracted from the total. For example: 8 errors: 2 points per error - total 16; mark out of 20: 4/20. Anything that the learner has done well is not taken into account. The positive aspect of the learner's work is not brought out, emphasis being placed on what has not worked. The learner knows what he is not capable of doing, which explains why all evaluation is perceived negatively and becomes a source of discouragement.

This way of considering evaluation, coupled with the practice of calculating the average of the marks obtained in various subjects, results in an evaluation which is devoid of all meaning.

How to remedy this situation? Proposals

The following practical proposals are the result of the work conducted by a working party on evaluation.

The ultimate aim of all evaluation is to assess the level of ability achieved and to determine whether it corresponds to the level required. It must permit the learner throughout his studies to assess his level in relation to precise objectives and requirements, to monitor his progress and work out what still has to be done to satisfy these requirements and attain these objectives. Evaluation can bear either on the extent of the learner's knowledge (the cognitive field) or on a level of competence more directly associated with the field of communication. Since it is the latter field that concerns us most, a definition will be given of levels of competence in the various fields of interest, viz comprehension and expression, to be evaluated separately.

1.   Separate evaluation of skills: observation of the way in which pupils learn indicates that progress is not made at the same rhythm in the various skills: the ability to understand, for example, develops more rapidly than the ability to express oneself. Accordingly, skills must be evaluated independently.

2.   Level of competence, definition of stages: the process of acquiring a skill may be divided into stages, and levels corresponding to the stages reached gradually throughout this process may also be specified. These stages are defined in relation to the knowledge of a specific content and to the capacity to manipulate this content for the purposes of communication. They can also be defined in relation to the course requirements which become increasingly stringent over the years, and enable learners to assess their level in relation to these requirements.

Three stages have been defined. Used to evaluate pupils as they finish school, they would enable examiners to specify the degree of competence achieved, while not questioning the concept of success or failure in an examination. This would make it possible simply to state that a certain candidate had passed - let us say the baccalauréat - that his results as a whole were such that he could be awarded the baccalauréat, while at the same time pointing out that in English he achieved such and such a stage. In this

way, it would be possible to specify the requirements for the baccalauréat.
For example, one could indicate the type of text to be read or listened to
(language difficulties, complexity of content, length of document to be
listened to; legibility of the text, level of comprehension - explicit and
implicit);the qualities of written expression (construction of discourse,
train of thought, quality of argument, richness of expression, stylistic
quality, etc); and the quality of oral expression (intelligibility, extent
of participation, reaction to the unexpected, choice of appropriate
structures, fluency, phonological qualities).

Definition of stages

The stages correspond to the degrees of language autonomy achieved, to
the degree to which pupils have acquired knowledge enabling them to
understand and express themselves.

PROFICIENCY STAGE (stage 1): the pupil has a good command of what he
has learnt. He is autonomous.

.   Comprehension of a written document. The candidate is able to understand
what he is reading, to grasp the key points of the text, to analyse the
pertinent details, appreciate the implicit, the import of the text and
formulate an opinion; he is also able to infer the meaning of words which
he does not know or recognise.

.   Comprehension of an oral document. The candidate is able to grasp the
key points of the message, understand the important details, appreciate the
references in the text, the implicit, the attitude of the speakers.

.   Oral expression. The candidate is able to make himself understood,
express his ideas clearly and appropriately, modulate his train of thought,
participate in conversation and take the initiative, to cope with the
unexpected, to «negotiate» and adapt himself to the speakers. Phonologically,
the rhythm, intonation, and stress are appropriate, his language is fluent.
Correct use of language.

.   Written expression. The candidate is able to express what he needs or
wants to convey in intelligible language. He knows how to construct his
text (coherence), and how to order his thoughts. His richness of expression
enables him to modulate his train of thought and adapt the register of the
language to suit the subject in question. Correct use of language.

THE CREDIT STAGE (stage 2): The pupil does not yet know how to exploit
everything he has learnt. Limited language autonomy.

.   Comprehension of a written document. The candidate is able to
understand the gist of the text, to grasp the essential, to appreciate most
of the important details of the document and deduce the meaning of the
words he does not know or recognise. He is still not able to appreciate
the implicit and references in the text.

.   Comprehension of an oral document. The candidate is able to grasp the
key points of the message, to understand enough detail to help him work
out the meaning and the attitude of the speakers.

.   <u>Written expression</u>. The candidate is able to make himself understood by using simple and appropriate language; he is able to construct, and make limited use of vocabulary restricted in quantity and quality.

.   <u>Oral expression</u>. The candidate is able to make himself understood in simple language, using acceptable intonation, stress and rhythm. He knows how to participate even if he does so clumsily. Vocabulary is not very varied but sufficient to enable the message to be understood by the speaker.

THRESHOLD STAGE (stage 3): The candidate is not yet truly autonomous with regard to language. This represents the minimum of knowledge required at a given level of study to allow the learner to progress.

.   <u>Written comprehension</u>. The candidate is just about able to identify a number of elements which will enable him to work out the meaning: characters, location, action, key points. The extent of his knowledge does not yet permit him to understand the important details.

.   <u>Oral comprehension</u>. The candidate only understands a few snatches of the message heard, some fragmentary statements. He understands the gist, but needs help to understand the message in more detail.

.   <u>Oral expression</u>. The candidate is just about able to produce fragmentary statements, to make himself understood more by extra-linguistic than by linguistic means, such as gestures. His language lacks accuracy, making it difficult to understand what he wants to convey.

.   <u>Written expression</u>. The candidate is able to write simple sentences in an approximative basic language which does not always correspond to what he intended to convey.

These proposals are designed to facilitate the learning of a foreign language by helping the learner to work out what level he is at. They can be used in a school curriculum, in adult education and for assessing performance in examinations. They permit considerable flexibility: a given stage could be required for a given certificate. Requirements may be made quite specific, with greater or lesser emphasis being placed on a particular field of competence. Thus, for a specific examination, the proficiency stage might be required in comprehension while the credit stage would be sufficient in expression.

These proposals could become applicable universally permitting a harmonisation of standards, so that the meaning and worth of a qualification could be readily appreciated.

CHAPTER III: A PROPOSAL FOR LANGUAGE EXCHANGE

SURVEY OF THE DEVELOPMENT OF ASSESSMENT TECHNIQUES
CONSISTENT WITH THE COMMUNICATIVE APPROACH

III.1 A STRATEGY FOR THE COLLECTION, STORAGE AND EXCHANGE
OF ASSESSMENT, EVALUATION AND EXAM APPROACHES AND INSTRUMENTS

---

by Rolf SCHÄRER
Eurocentre, Zurich, Switzerland

Assessment has a vital place in any teaching and learning process and especially so in the area of foreign languages. Since traditional techniques of assessment often seem to conflict with the building up of communicative competence a major effort is needed to bring assessment procedures into harmony with this aim.

To develop ideas and principles is one step, to disseminate them widely, to get them shared and accepted another.

When, as is the case with the Modern Languages Project, the implementation involves thousands of independent agents and people throughout Europe, monitoring of progress and exchange of information and know-how in key areas becomes vital for a balanced and cost-effective development.

Therefore it is suggested that a format to collect and exchange information on assessment be created which allows computerised storage and retrieval.

1. Goal: to develop a framework which stimulates and allows:

1.1 the collection, storage and retrieval of assessment, evaluation, tests and exam instruments as well as descriptions of approaches and experiments related to the project;

1.2 the exchange of this information between interested and authorised institutions and persons;

1.3 the transfer of know-how and instruments to support further development.

2. Guiding principles

Those who work on communicative assessment will be encouraged to contribute information on their work on the following lines:

2.1 there will be a standard format for the description which contains all subsequent search headings;

2.2 information on assessment and evaluation procedures from projects supported by the CDCC will be stored and made available compulsorily;

2.3 the authors or copyright holders of other projects and instruments alone decide what and how much they want to make available;

2.4 there will be no screening of entries, the judgement of the author for the initial entry or of the user(s) for additional entries being accepted without question;

2.5 there will not be any super data bank to which all information is fed, but individual institutions will be encouraged to use the common framework to build up those sections of the information relevant and useful to them;

2.6 only a register of participating institutions will be made available centrally.

3. Strategy for collection, storage and exchange

Assessment, evaluation and exams affect everyone involved in the teaching and learning process. At different times different people might find different information useful and valuable. Hence the strategy should be to collect, store and exchange openly as much information as possible.

In this field confidentiality however is often crucial for the maintenance of credibility and therefore information can only be disclosed as far as it does not harm the purpose of an approach or instrument. Hence the strategy must be to collect and store information in a way that access to it can be controlled.

Some users like ministries will need mainly global and strategic information; others like teachers will need detailed and practical help. For them speed of access will be a more important factor than for users with more global needs. Hence the framework has to be built up to satisfy both global and detailed access.

4. Target groups

Possible target groups in order of absolute size are:

a. learners (L)
b. teachers (T)
c. teacher trainers (TT)
d. materials writers (MW)
e. researchers and testers (RD)
f. ministries of education and local authorities (Min)

5. <u>Primary information need for each group</u>

Target group Info need	L	T	TT	MW	RD	Min
assessment philosophy				*		*
evaluation strategy				*	*	*
forms of assessment		*	*	*	*	*
evaluation systems					*	*
evaluation tools		*	*	*		
resources needed						*
social impact					*	*
validity/reliability				*	*	*
procedures		*				*
training requirements			*			*
availability		*		*	*	*
sample tests	*	*			*	
self evaluation	*	*			*	
marking schemes		*			*	
exam systems	*	*			*	*
exam values	*					*
exam options	*					
exam costs	*					*
purpose of instrument						
diagnoses		*				
ranking		*				*
progress measurement		*				
final measurement	*	*				*
certification	*					*
statistical information					*	*
results of experiments						
on learning					*	
on teaching					*	
on formative eval.		*	*	*	*	
on summative eval.					*	*
evaluation results						
on learners	*	*			*	
on teachers		*	*		*	
on materials		*		*	*	
on learning system					*	*
on evaluation system					*	
on backwash effects		*	*		*	*
on social impact		*			*	*

This table clearly shows that there will be a mass of information out of which only a small part will be relevant and of interest to a particular user at any given time.

Any framework to be developed should therefore only be seen as a tool and lead to a network of information banks which can be adapted and modified to the needs of different users.

The following paper (cf III.2) provides a sample format of a possible realisation.

III.2 AUTOMATIC DATA PROCESSING:
AN EXAMPLE OF A SYSTEM USING A DATA BASE

by Paul Mairesse
Eurocentre, Zurich, Switzerland

For several years, tests and examinations devised by many public, private or semi-public institutions in the member states of the Council for Cultural Co-operation of the Council of Europe have been influenced by the communicative approach, although in different degrees and some time after the advent of communicative methods themselves. It is therefore becoming necessary to assess the extent of this change. However, the salient features of this trend are the lack of co-ordination between different schemes and their heterogeneous nature. It really does seem that «something is going on» at present in the field of assessment, but it is difficult to measure the scale of this change and analyse its nature. To describe what is taking place it is necessary both to draw up an inventory of the schemes mentioned above and to design ways of making a comparative analysis of them. Finally, it must also be pointed out that, as this is likely to take several years, it must be an ongoing activity with new data fed in continuously.

All of this suggests that it is essential to design a method of computer processing of the data collected during such a project. Firstly, because the volume of information is so large that an effective system must be adopted both for record-keeping purposes and the exploitation of the information. Secondly, because the main feature of such a method is its flexibility in use: it is possible not only to update the information at any moment, but also to change the processing operation easily. The latter point is very important because the criteria or distinctive categories used to pick out significant differences between ways of assessing proficiency are very likely to undergo considerable change. Some trends which are already beginning to emerge, such as the movement away from the traditional distinction between the four skill areas (expression/comprehension/oral/ written) in favour of an integrated approach, or the emergence of complex tasks with a tendency to replace multiple-choice questionnaires, texts with gaps and the like, are the first signs of this change, which must be anticipated if it is to be mastered.

The systematic collection and updating of the information is in itself a colossal undertaking (to give only one example, about thirty different groups are currently working in the United Kingdom on unit credit systems). Such systematic collection and updating is nevertheless essential in order to be able to give an account of developments in the field of assessment and to form an accurate picture of trends which are emerging. In any case, the collection and updating cannot be started until the definitive version of the system for processing and exploiting the data has been worked out.

2.   Proposals for the organisational details of the survey

The survey to collect the necessary information for the project has two distinct phases: the collection of the basic data and the analysis of the assessment systems recorded.

2.1 Collection of the basic data

The idea is to conduct a survey among test designers, who are requested to provide a copy of all the assessment material and fill in the corresponding questionnaires (Appendices 1 to 3). As a preliminary measure it will be necessary to identify and list those people/contacts who can provide this information.

2.2 Evaluation

This will involve all the data collected from test designers and could be supplemented if necessary by comments from different users (see Appendix 5). The evaluation grid (Appendix 4) is intended to provide a profile of the test in the light of the data mentioned above. It will be noted that it goes back over a number of the points contained in the questionnaires, but for a significantly different purpose: the aim here is not to provide raw information, but rather to define the position of a particular assessment system in relation to a series of options expressed in each case in terms of more or less mutually exclusive approaches, and which we have good reason to suppose are key elements in the field of communicative competence. It is not, however, intended to identify the criteria which might be used to decide whether this or that test deserves to be described as "communicative", but rather, more modestly, to provide a basis for assessing whether the test in question is appropriate to a particular teaching situation. Individuals or groups who are asked to fill it in will be able to use it to express opinions which will differ considerably, depending on their objectives, their concerns and their own scale of values.

3. Organisation of the database

STRUCTURE OF THE DATABASE

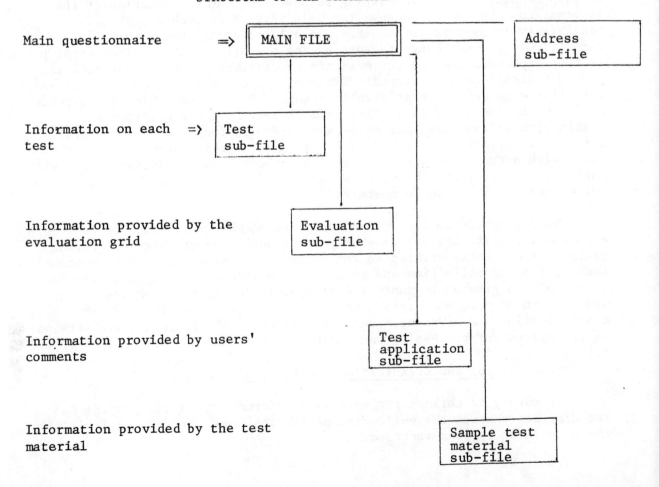

Main questionnaire ⇒	MAIN FILE
	Address sub-file
Information on each ⇒ test	Test sub-file
Information provided by the evaluation grid	Evaluation sub-file
Information provided by users' comments	Test application sub-file
Information provided by the test material	Sample test material sub-file

The above diagram gives some idea of the way the database is organised. In developing this system a number of principles, referred to very briefly below, were taken into account.

It will be noted first of all that the information is not collected in a single file but is divided up into a series of sub-files, each separate from the others but all linked to a main file through which access to them is controlled. This system serves the dual purpose of avoiding a waste of memory space and controlling access to the information more easily. It may also be observed that separate files correspond to equally separate sources of information. This is because a very close connection must exist between survey methods (questionnaires etc) and the corresponding input procedures. Finally, it should be noted that there is an address sub-file which occupies a separate position within the structure. The information contained in this file makes it possible to computerise the procedures for regular correspondence with the contacts who provide the input for the database.

4. Updating of the database

A distinction should be drawn between updating of the content, or routine updating, and updating of the structure, or special updating.

Routine updating is carried out by means of a group of programmes controlled by a menu system. Use of these programmes requires only a very elementary knowledge of data processing, because the software employed, Ashton Tate's DBASE III, uses a programming language which permits this sort of application. Routine updating involves both the input of new information and the management of the system of regular correspondence with contacts.

Special updating is a partial modification of the file structure. Such a modification may prove to be necessary when some of the descriptive categories used have lost their relevance or when new descriptive categories become essential in order to reflect a change in assessment methods. This type of modification can only be carried out in command mode and requires the correction of quite a large number of related "command programmes". It therefore calls for a very good knowledge of programming and of the architecture of the database. The initial choice of categories must be very carefully made in order to postpone the need for such a change as long as possible.

5. Exploitation of the database

The first function of the database is obviously to centralise and accumulate information. But this accumulation will be useful only if it leads to exploitation of the information. Exploitation means procedures for the extraction of information which make it possible to form an opinion or assist with decision-making, as the case may be. On this last point, it should be made clear that a rationally exploited database is not an expert system and that too much should not be expected of it.

One type of enquiry is a comprehensive one, corresponding in human language to the request "tell me everything you know". The result is a more or less exhaustive and variously organised list of the contents. This is a rather crude type of enquiry, but it is nevertheless sometimes useful.

A second type is a selective enquiry which consists in searching for information on the basis of one or more criteria. This type of enquiry can meet particular requirements for information on the existence or nature of this or that type of assessment material.

A third type of enquiry is a contrastive enquiry intended to identify systematically the differences between different sets of information in the database. It is possible to decide how systematic the comparison is to be, and it may involve as much or as little of the contents as one wishes.

The last type is the enquiry into trends or developments. With the software used it is possible to carry out a quantitative interpretation of the contents in the form of either a synchronic or a diachronic study. This is perhaps the most fruitful and most useful type of enquiry, as it goes beyond a simple statement of fact and can provide information on constant factors or observable changes over a specific period.

It should be noted that not all these different ways of consulting the database can be computerised to the same extent, as some of them create more programming problems than others.

Finally, the reliability of the results obtained will depend directly on the representativity of the contents, which is in turn linked to the scale of the survey and the goodwill of those people who agree to help with it.

o

o   o

Appendix 1

Assessment systems and communicative competence

MAIN QUESTIONNAIRE

I. IDENTIFICATION

- TITLE:

- REFERENCE:

- AUTHOR(S):

- INSTITUTION:

- NAME AND ADDRESS OF CONTACT: ....

- DATE:

- LANGUAGE:

- FIELD:

2. FUNCTION

- TARGET GROUP:

- LEVEL:

- TYPE:

      ☐ a.   Test

      ☐ b.   Examination

      ☐ c.   Certificate

      ☐ d.   Internal assessment system

        Other:

      ☐ ....

- FUNCTION:

☐ a. Aptitude

☐ b. Placement

☐ c. Summative assessment

☐ d. Formative assessment

Other

☐ ....

3. GENERAL INFORMATION

- TEST DURATION:

- STAFF REQUIRED:

- DEGREE OF TRAINING REQUIRED:

- MARKING SCHEME:

- MARKING TIME PER PUPIL:

- THEORETICAL BASIS OF TEST:

- ASSOCIATED METHOD:

- ASSOCIATED MATERIAL (log book, progress sheet, etc):

- DOCUMENTS ENCLOSED:

☐ Presentation booklet

☐ Associated scheme of work

Appendix 2

DESIGN PRINCIPLES

1. Is the main objective of the assessment system to measure:

    ☐ Knowledge of structures and vocabulary

    ☐ Is the assessment system designed for a restricted target group with special features?

2. Is the assessment system designed for a restricted target group with special features?

    ☐ Yes

    ☐ No

    If so, what are these features?

3. Which different language skills are taken into account? (Please state the relative importance of each skill.)

Time (%)	Final mark (%)		Skill
			Written expression
			Oral expression
			Reading comprehension
			Listening comprehension
			Other (please specify)
			....
			....
			....
			....

4. Are these different skills assessed by means of separate activities?

☐ Yes

☐ No

5. What steps are taken to ensure

a. The reliability of the assessment system?

....

b. The validity of the assessment system?

....

(Validity: the assessment system actually measures what it is
supposed to measure

Statistical reliability: the results of any one test are comparable
with those of other applications of the same test)

6. Are the support or reference materials used in the tests (1) usually
authentic documents?

☐ Yes

☐ No

If so, are they presented in their original form?

☐ Yes

☐ No

7. Do the tasks set have a practical, functional purpose?

☐ Yes

☐ No

If so, do the instructions make it clear in what contexts the
tasks are supposed to be carried out.

☐ Yes

☐ No

---

(1) Main material

8.   Which of the following different types of questions are used?

☐   True-false

☐   Multiple choice

☐   Gapped script

☐   Pairing exercise

☐   Re-ordering

☐   Open-ended questions

☐   Conversations, interviews

☐   Role playing, structured interaction

☐   Longer oral or written presentation
    (letter, report, summary, etc)

☐   Other (please specify)

☐   ....

☐   ....

☐   ....

9. Does the test use authentic documents to make the pupils' answers a direct response to a real situation?

    ☐ Yes

    ☐ No

10. Is the assessment

    ☐ Criterion-referenced?

    ☐ Norm-referenced?

11. What criteria are taken into consideration in the assessment of the pupils' work, in order of importance?

    ....
    ....
    ....
    ....

12. Comments/further details:

    ....
    ....
    ....
    ....

Appendix 3

Assessment systems and communicative competence

INFORMATION ON EACH TEST USED

Title of the test: ....

Reference: ....

Language skill assessed: ....

Description of the activity:

....
....
....

Comment on the format of the test:

....
....
....

Type(s) of question used: ....

Linguistic material on which the activity is based

Nature: ....
Type: ....
Origin: ....
Function: ....
Thematic content: ....

Technical and material aspects:

....
....

Sum up in two lines the marking criteria and the marking scheme ....
....
....

Comments/further details: ....
....

Appendix 4

No.	Objectives (left pole)	Scale	Objectives (right pole)
1.	Objectives		Objectives
1.1	Skill(s) assessed: knowledge of the rules of the language	⟷	Skill(s) assessed: ability to communicate, language proficiency corresponding to particular requirements
1.2	Based on identification of the specific features of the target language	⟷	Based on identification of the learners' social and communication requirements
1.3	Aspects of competence taken into account: reduced to a minimum number of elements considered significant	⟷	Aspects of competence taken into account: numerous (comprehension/expression/oral/ written – all-round proficiency)
1.4	Statistical reliability (1) based on psychometric data	⟷	Reliability of the test ensured by detailed marking scheme (1)
1.5	Validity (2) based on extraneous, objective psychometric data	⟷	Validity based on a precise definition of what the test is supposed to measure
2.	Material on which the activities are based (3)		Material on which the activities are based
2.1	Nature: specifically prepared by test designers for the particular requirements of assessment	⟷	Nature: authentic or realistic
2.2	Presentation: standardised	⟷	Presentation: importance attached to realism
3.	Tasks		Tasks
3.1	Nature: activities specific to the assessment of knowledge	⟷	Nature: functional, practical
3.2	Form of instructions: tasks independent of any particular context	⟷	Form of instructions: tasks placed in context
3.3	Type of answer required: standardised forms of expression	⟷	Type of answer required: non-standardised forms of expression
3.4	Nature of the test material: wholly produced by the test designers	⟷	Nature of the test material: authentic or realistic
4.	Assessment criteria		Assessment criteria
4.1	Norm-referenced test	⟷	Criterion-referenced test
4.2	Total objectivity claimed for the test	⟷	Recognition of the part played by subjectivity in the assessment
4.3	Emphasis on: accurate use of the language	⟷	Emphasis on: fluency, ease of expression

(1) Comparability of results obtained on different occasions in spite of variations in test conditions

(2) The test actually measures what it is supposed to measure

(3) Training material and/or examples of marked work

Appendix 5

Assessment systems and communicative competence

TEST USERS COMMENTS

Test: ....

User: ....

Institution: ....

Target group: ....

Circumstances and aim of the test: ....
....
....
....
....
....

Results: ....
....
....
....

Interest shown by the pupils: ....

Presentation: ....

Practical details: ....

Overall approval: ....
....
....
....

APPENDIX I

CONCLUSIONS AND RECOMMENDATIONS OF THE MEETING OF EXPERTS ON TESTING, ASSESSMENT AND EVALUATION (STRASBOURG, 26-27 JUNE 1986)

1.   Authorities responsible for examinations and tests are recommended to take account of the following considerations in their work:

-   the need to rethink carefully the traditionally important criteria of validity, objectivity, discrimination and reliability in the context of the learning and teaching of languages for communication;

-   the need to ensure that guidelines and regulations for evaluation, assessment and testing respect the individual learner's personality and identity;

-   the logistic, financial and personal constraints upon teachers and other testers in operating «communicative» teaching procedures;

-   the need for tests of communicative competence to encompass social and personal as well as linguistic competence;

-   the fact that each test or battery of test items constructs its own social reality, which is decisive for what is «significant» for the tester, institution and society concerned;

-   the various levels at which evaluation takes place and the variety of needs it serves for different users.

2.   Further research and development is needed:

-   to develop clear criteria for the grading of texts and tasks;

-   to determine the place of grammar and culture in a communicative approach;

-   to develop tools for the evaluation of communicative strategies (productive and receptive).

3.   The Council for Cultural Co-operation should promote:

a.   the publication of a special booklet on «Communicative language testing» of limited size, in several languages, directed towards teachers and teacher trainers. This booklet should be based on the papers presented in June 1986 and contain the following sections:

   i.   the educational context of testing

      -   the principle of communicative language teaching

      -   understanding the learner (learner psychology, autonomy, etc)

      -   testing as an educational option, (eg as an aid to the negotiation of learning objectives, strategies, methods and materials)

ii.   the functions of testing

iii. the effects of testing (psychological effects on learners and teachers, backwash effects on classroom activities)

iv.   quality criteria

v.   the production and use of evaluation tools in the foreign language classroom

vi.   an index of suitable materials and further information about contact persons

vii. a selected, annotated bibliography;

b.   the development of autonomous evaluation strategies, particularly strategies for the self-assessment of communicative ability;

c.   the collection and dissemination of information on projects at national level concerned with communicative foreign language teaching. This might involve the establishment of a data bank (cf. the paper by Mr R. SCHÄRER).

A P P E N D I X II

INDEX OF CONTRIBUTORS TO THE REPORT/INDEX DES CONTRIBUTEURS AU RAPPORT

Mr Michael BUCKBY, Director, Language Teaching Centre,
University of York, Heslington, York, YO1 5DD,
UNITED KINGDOM/ROYAUME-UNI.

Mr Viljo KOHONEN, Head of the Department of Teacher Education,
University of Tampere, P.O. Box 607, 33101 Tampere, 10,
FINLAND/FINLANDE.

Mr Paul MAIRESSE, EUROCENTRES - Fondation for European Language and Educational
Centres, Seestrasse 247, 8038 Zurich,
SWITZERLAND/SUISSE.

Mme Jane SAMUEL, Ex chef de la Section langues vivantes de l'INRP,
Parc Eiffel, 92310 Sèvres,
FRANCE.

Mr Rolf SCHÄRER, Director, EUROCENTRES - Fondation for European Language and
Educational Centres, Seestrasse 247, 8038 Zurich,
SWITZERLAND/SUISSE.

Dr. Michael SCHRATZ, Institut für Erziehungswissenschaften der Universität
Innsbruck, Innrain 52/V, 6020 Innsbruck, AM,
AUSTRIA/AUTRICHE.

Dr. Mats OSKARSSON, Department of Education and Educational Research,
Gothenburg University, Box 1010, 431 26 Mölndal,
SWEDEN/SUEDE.

Dr. John L.M. TRIM, Adviser to the Council of Europe, Modern Languages Project,
53 Barrow Road, Cambridge CB2 2AR,
UNITED KINGDOM/ROYAUME-UNI.

Dr Jan van WEEREN, Head of the Language Department, National Institute for
Educational Measurement, CITO, Nieuwer Oeverstraat 65, P.O. Box 1034,
6801 MG Arnhem,
NETHERLANDS/PAYS-BAS.

SALES AGENTS FOR PUBLICATIONS
OF THE COUNCIL OF EUROPE